BILLIE JEAN KING · ARTHUR ASHE · STAN
NAVRATILOVA · TRACY
VENUS AND SERENA WILLIA
JACK KRAMER · MAUREEN CONNOLLY · PA
KING · ARTHUR ASHE · STAN SMITH ·
NAVRATILOVA · TRACY AUSTIN · JOHN MCEN
AND SERENA WILLIAMS · BILL TILDEN ·
MAUREEN CONNOLLY · PANCHO GON
ARTHUR ASHE · STAN SMITH · CHRIS EVERT
TRACY AUSTIN · JOHN MCENROE · PETE SAM
WILLIAMS · BILL TILDEN · HELEN WILLS MO
CONNOLLY · PANCHO GONZALEZ · ALTHEA
STAN SMITH · CHRIS EVERT · JIMMY CONN
JOHN MCENROE · PETE SAMPRAS · ANDRE
TILDEN · HELEN WILLS MOODY · DON BUDG
GONZALEZ · ALTHEA GIBSON · BILLIE JEA
CHRIS EVERT · JIMMY CONNORS · MARTINA NAVRA
PETE SAMPRAS · ANDRE AGASSI · VENUS AND S
MOODY · DON BUDGE · JACK KRAMER · MA
GIBSON · BILLIE JEAN KING · ARTHUR
CONNORS · MARTINA NAVRATILOVA · TRACY

The
IMMORTALS
of American Tennis

Emirates Airline
CITIZEN
1:35

The

IMMORTALS

of American Tennis

Steve Flink

GELDING STREET PRESS

A Gelding Street Press book
An imprint of Rockpool Publishing
PO Box 252
Summer Hill
NSW 2130 Australia

geldingstreetpress.com
Follow us! ◙ Geldingstreet_press

ISBN: 9781922662323

Published in 2026 by Gelding Street Press

Design and typesetting by Maddie Egremont, Rockpool Publishing
Edited by Kathy Hassett

Front cover: Top row (left to right): *Billie Jean King at Wimbledon
in 1962; Bill Tilden circa 1920; Arthur Ashe at Wimbledon in 1975.
Bottom row (left to right): Pete Sampras in 1994; Serena Williams
at the 2013 US Open; Chris Evert at the 1985 US Open.*

Back cover: *Andre Agassi at the 1990 French Open.*

Endpapers: *Don Budge at Wimbledon in 1937.*

Printed and bound in China

Dedication

For my friend S.L. Price, a singularly versatile and
elegant sportswriter, a craftsman through and through,
and the most generous of all my colleagues.

CONTENTS

INTRODUCTION

The incomparable game of tennis – originally known as "lawn tennis" – was born long ago in Great Britain, back in the spring of 1874. The Welshman Major Walter Clopton Wingfield was the inventor of the modern form of the sport, which had been preceded by the indoor game "real tennis". Tennis swiftly established a prominence in England. Three years later, the first edition of Wimbledon – officially known then and now as "The Championships" – took place on the pristine grass courts of the All England Croquet and Lawn Tennis Club. Four years after that, the inaugural United States Championships was held at Newport, Rhode Island. By 1905, the Australasian Championships (renamed the Australian Championships in 1927) was established. Soon it became a revered international event, and the French Championships followed officially on the worldwide calendar starting in 1925 after many years as strictly a national competition.

Those four tournaments and each of their nations took tennis unswervingly into the future, eventually becoming known as the "Grand Slam" tournaments – or "majors". In the latter stages of the 19th century, tennis found a foothold in the sports universe, capturing the imagination of the public, creating legions of fans and participants, growing steadily wherever it was played.

The game kept evolving, but most historians agree that tennis soared to another level altogether starting in the 1920s. That was a landmark decade in all of sports, with Jack Dempsey a standout performer in boxing, Bobby Jones gracing the game of golf, the charismatic slugger Babe Ruth inspiring baseball fans as an iconic New York Yankee, and the first authentic superstars of tennis rising toward immortality. That is why the first players selected for this book are those that came of age in the twenties.

Until 1968, only amateurs were permitted to play in the four major championships. But that year, "Open Tennis" at long last emerged, allowing amateurs and professionals to compete against each other in the same tournaments. Six of the luminaries featured in this book competed in the pre-Open years, nine came along after the advent of Open Tennis, and four more appeared in the amateur years before becoming professionals and standouts in the Open Era.

The first immortal tennis players from the United States emerged over the course of the 1920s as Bill Tilden and Helen Wills made their presence known not only among their game's giants and tennis fans but also to the broader public, establishing themselves as early sporting celebrities.

In decade after decade across the twentieth century, American tennis players featured prominently on the world's premier stages. For the purposes of this book, my list of American immortals includes only 19 players – ten men and nine women. But I had to leave out many individuals who were entirely worthy of consideration, which was no simple task. The players who narrowly missed the cut are included in the Honorable Mentions chapter.

What makes me qualified to make these tough judgments and determine the elite group of competitors whom you will be reading about in the chapters ahead?

My passion for tennis started in 1965, when I was 12 and went to Wimbledon for the first time. From that day forward I followed the sport fervently. By the time I was 15, my goal was to establish myself as a tennis reporter. In my late teens and early twenties, I worked behind the scenes with two estimable journalists, Bud Collins from the U.S. and John Barrett of Great Britain, in the early 1970s. Both were not only leading print reporters, but also top-of-the-line television broadcasters. I tried to put my photographic memory to good use in assisting them behind the scenes.

When I was 22, after my junior year at Stetson University in Florida, I accepted a full-time position as a writer and editor at *World Tennis* magazine in New York, a dream job if ever there was one. I had been reading that esteemed publication every month for eight years. I remained there for no fewer than 17 years, and then spent 15 years writing for *Tennis Week* magazine. Since that time, I have contributed regularly to various websites and weighed in on the most potent topics in tennis.

Meanwhile, I wrote three books between 1999 and 2020 that all have related to the history of the game. As a self-effacing man who does not like calling attention to myself, I am not fond of carrying on about my credentials. But I want everyone who reads this book to realize that I have spent most of my lifetime devoted to tennis. So it is my sincere hope that if you disagree with any of my selections – or believe I left someone out who in your view belongs in the book – that you do so agreeably and respectfully. I have thought long and hard about which Americans are worthy of wearing the label of immortality. I have interviewed many of the players featured in these pages frequently over the past half century, and have spoken with a number of them recently to have the benefit of their reflections long after retiring from the sport.

The tennis players in this book have, without exception, achieved stupendously, flourishing when it has mattered the most, defining themselves as larger-than-life figures with their prodigious feats. Some were on top of the sport for longer than others. Each has a unique set of attributes. All have lived under the banner of greatness. They are champions with unassailable reputations and breathtaking bodies of work, individuals who irrevocably altered tennis in their country and around the world, and immensely important figures who changed the face of tennis significantly in one way or another. They are legendary athletes who will live forever in our hearts and minds. They are immortals.

The United States has arguably given the game more immortals than any other country. As this book goes to print, there are four American women – Serena Williams, Helen Wills Moody, Chris Evert and Martina Navratilova – among the top five all-time major singles champions. The first player ever to secure a Grand Slam by sweeping all four majors in a calendar year was Don Budge of the United States, and since his time many of the American male players have established themselves as household names – including Pancho Gonzalez, Arthur Ashe, Jimmy Connors,

Tracy Austin – playing in a senior invitational at the U.S. Open at age 50 – keeps her eyes glued to the ball as if still in her prime.

John McEnroe, Pete Sampras, and Andre Agassi. I have written about these standouts comprehensively in the pages that follow. It is my hope that you will enjoy re-examining a number of very familiar American icons who have surely enriched your lives with their heroics, while getting to know more about some estimable players who may not be as well-known but also belong in that exclusive territory of immortals.

Steve Flink

Tilden in the early 1920s executing the improved backhand that transformed his career.

Bill Tilden

Full name	William Tatem Tilden II
Birthdate	10 February 1893; died 5 June 1953
Place of birth	Philadelphia, Pennsylvania
Major singles titles	7 U.S. Championships (1920–25, 1929); 3 Wimbledon (1920–1921, 1930)

The champion who defined immortality in the landscape of American tennis more persuasively than anyone else, "Big Bill" Tilden was a transformational figure.

At a time when tennis was exploding with popularity, Tilden was the central player and dominant force across the 1920s and beyond, capturing the public imagination, stamping his authority on the game with singular will and shotmaking virtuosity, establishing himself unassailably as a craftsman of the highest order and a clinician who left no stone unturned in his pursuit of excellence on the court. His was a quest to move however close he could to the edge of perfection. Tilden amassed ten major singles titles over the course of his sterling career, taking more of these prizes than any other American man has ever done save Pete Sampras.

To be sure, a number of formidable male players from the United States had taken the court in the four decades prior to Tilden's rise. Richard "Dick" Sears secured the first seven U.S. National Championship titles from 1881–87. Bill Larned replicated that feat with seven victories at "The Nationals" between 1901 and 1911. Maurice McLoughlin, known in tennis circles as the "California Comet", was the standout American in 1912–13 and a potent striker of the ball with an explosive serve to boot.

But it was Tilden with his masterful skills who would turn tennis upside down and become the first superstar among the Americans. He was an unmistakably charismatic performer

In a landmark 1921 season, Tilden was victorious at Wimbledon and the U.S. Championships, and led the Americans to a Davis Cup triumph.

who wanted to be acclaimed not only for winning prestigious tournaments but also for achieving on his own terms with unsurpassed majesty and distinctive flair.

In contrast with so many other luminaries in the tennis universe who started to at least approach the peak of their powers by their early twenties, Tilden took longer to grow into his talent and propel himself into the hierarchy of the game.

The turning point for this inimitable competitor was the year 1920. He had spent the previous two seasons ranked second in the United States, but Tilden realized he sorely needed to address a serious vulnerability in his game. His backhand was decidedly weaker than his forehand, and so in late 1919 he took about six months off from competition to revamp his backhand and turn it into a more productive and punishing stroke.

That audacious move provided Tilden with some much-needed inner security and added the last layer of stability to his arsenal. As he headed into the heart of the 1920 season, Tilden realized that his adversaries no longer had an avenue to exploit him from the back of the court. Now Tilden was masterful off both wings and that, combined with the speed and accuracy of his serve, made him virtually unbeatable.

He went to London in the summer of 1920 determined to capture the world's premier title on the British lawns, and succeeded, establishing himself as the first American man ever to capture the title at Wimbledon. It was a career-altering moment for a man with the highest of aspirations. In the final, he defeated the defending champion Gerald Patterson of Australia in four sets. At 27, knowing he was approaching the peak of his powers, Tilden had collected his first Grand Slam title.

Buoyed by that triumph, he capped off that summer with a second straight major championship victory. In a stirring five-set final at the U.S. Championships on the fabled grass courts at the West Side Tennis Club in Forest Hills, New York, "Big Bill" Tilden took the crown away from "Little Bill" Johnston. A year earlier in the same stadium, Johnston had dismissed Tilden easily in straight sets when they collided in the final round. But this was a different Tilden. "Big Bill" had surpassed "Little Bill" and both players realized that a sea change had taken place.

At the end of that memorable season, Tilden led the United States to victory in the Davis Cup's 20th anniversary year. Tilden's trifecta of triumphs at Wimbledon, the U.S. Championships, and in the Davis Cup was striking evidence of his growing authority.

As the 1920s progressed, Tilden built success upon success, turning tennis into his kingdom, enlarging the sport immeasurably in the public eye, raising his stature every step of the way. Year after year, he mastered his craft and increasingly distanced himself from the rest of the field. In 1921, Tilden defended his Wimbledon crown with a final-round comeback win over the South African Brian Norton. Tilden later asserted in his 1948 memoir, *My Story*, that when he got back to the clubhouse afterwards, exhausted and not feeling well, he collapsed. He trailed two sets to love in that contest but altered his tactics, slowing down the pace of the match and slicing his shots judiciously to disrupt his opponent's rhythm. Tilden battled ferociously to reach a fifth set and then saved two match points at the tail end of the encounter to prevail 4-6, 2-6, 6-1, 6-0, 7-5.

Many believed Tilden deliberately manufactured danger in significant matches like his battle with Norton, knowing he could rally from the brink of defeat and thus garner the affection of the crowds who witnessed these dramatic turnarounds. As *New York Times* journalist Allison Danzig wrote, "The tennis court became a stage. He was in love with it and with the crowds … To win them on his side, he went to lengths that seemed to border on lunacy. He would allow his opponent to gain so big a lead as to make his own defeat appear inevitable."

In any case, whether he won decisively or rallied from the brink of defeat, Tilden felt invincible. He took the U.S. Championships again in the summer of 1921 at the Germantown Cricket Club in Philadelphia where he was born and raised. The following year, he made it three in a row, claiming the title with another of his trademark comebacks from two sets down against "Little Bill".

But the gap between "Little Bill" and "Big Bill" widened considerably in 1923, when Tilden took apart Johnston 6-4, 6-1, 6-4 in the final of the U.S. Championships. A year later, Tilden retained the title with a masterful 6-1, 9-7,

6-2 final-round win over Johnston. At 30, brimming with confidence, unhesitating in his conviction when the stakes were greatest, understanding his match-playing capacities better than he ever had before, Tilden was surely at his absolute zenith.

And yet, he had some substantial years ahead. In 1925, playing with a sore shoulder and plainly hampered by the ailment, Tilden toppled Johnston once more to take his sixth U.S. Championships title in a row, overcoming his compatriot in five sets. Although Tilden would remain at the top of American tennis through 1929 – completing a record ten years in a row as the No. 1 ranked player in his nation – his supremacy was never again as far reaching. Tilden secured only two more major championships, collecting his seventh and last U.S. Championships in 1929 and then winning his third Wimbledon singles title in 1930. In the former tournament, he survived five-set skirmishes with countrymen John Doeg and Frank Hunter, and in the latter he defeated fellow American Wilmer Allison to become the second-oldest man ever to rule on the British lawns at the age of 37.

Tilden ended his amateur career upon the conclusion of that 1930 season, having demonstrated an utter command of his craft. Toward the end of those amateur years, however, he had been having increasing difficulty overcoming two

Tilden congratulates Rene Lacoste after one of their riveting duels in 1927 when the Frenchman took the No. 1 world ranking from the American.

estimable members of the famed "Four Musketeers" from France. Rene Lacoste and Henri Cochet were thorns in his side in the late twenties. Lacoste upended Tilden in a tumultuous five-set final at the 1927 French Championships in Paris, prevailing 11-9 in the fifth set after Tilden twice advanced to match point when ahead 9-8. Only a few weeks later, Tilden collapsed after leading by two sets to love and 5-1 in the third set against Cochet, who would collect 17 points in a row and eventually win 2-6, 4-6, 7-5, 6-4, 6-3 in the penultimate round at Wimbledon. Lacoste upended Tilden again 11-9, 6-3, 11-9 in the final of the 1927 U.S. Championships.

Meanwhile, Tilden would lose to Lacoste in the semifinals of Wimbledon in 1928 and in the same round at the French Championships in 1929. A few weeks later he was toppled by Cochet at Wimbledon. Cochet and Lacoste each garnered seven majors in singles across their scintillating careers. They were prolific performers. But Tilden losing to that extraordinary pair of champions so many times on auspicious occasions was evidence of his slight decline.

The imperious Tilden was almost unbeatable across the first half of the 1920s.

The rising mastery of the Frenchmen was also evident in the Davis Cup. For four straight years, from 1927–30, they stopped the United States in the Challenge Round. In that span, Tilden

was beaten once by Lacoste and three times by Cochet as the gifted and powerfully driven Frenchmen hit their zeniths while Tilden was moving past his prime. Addressing Cochet in *My Story*, Tilden wrote, "He was the only man who beat me more than I beat him as an amateur. Only after he turned professional did I overhaul his lead and build up a comfortable lead for myself."

While Tilden was enduring some arduous times in his rivalries with the Frenchmen, he was also often feuding with umpires and officials at various tournaments, creating numerous scenes as if to suggest that he was a transcendent champion who did not need to play by the conventional rules but could instead make up his own. He also was often at odds with the officers of the United States Lawn Tennis Association (later renamed United States Tennis Association). They found Tilden in violation of their rules when he wrote tennis articles for newspapers and suspended him in 1928 for that transgression.

Some observers believed that Tilden's tempestuous behavior on the court was because "Big Bill" could only operate at peak efficiency and get the most out of his competitive resources if he severely disparaged umpires, linesmen and referees who made decisions with which he took exception. One such authority on Tilden was Al Laney of the

New York Herald Tribune, who eventually joined the aforementioned Allison Danzig of the *New York Times* in the International Tennis Hall of Fame.

Laney wrote in his book *Covering the Court*, "Tilden remained to the end of his career just as mercurial as he had been in his rise to world supremacy. He seemed to have learned that when he tried to curb his temperament, to rein it in, he lost matches … Tilden became the greatest of champions because he could turn creative artistry into unparalleled performance."

As Laney observed frequently, Tilden defined himself as a champion with a theatricality unlike any of his peers. He would be consumed by anger and still unleash tennis that surely no one else could have summoned under such circumstances.

It seemed that Tilden not only commanded attention for his extraordinary exploits on the court, but he wanted to be noticed away from the arena, even if that meant it would reflect poorly on him. Nonetheless, he was revered in the tennis community and amongst fellow players because he was not only an iconic player but also a genius who studied the game as deeply as anyone ever had, and later wrote three outstanding instructional books on the sport that were revelatory for the depth of his insights and the clarity of his mind.

But Tilden was irrefutably a complicated man, sometimes drawn to conflict inexplicably, tormented in many ways. In the latter stages of his life, he would be twice arrested and sent to prison in 1947 and again in 1949 on morals charges involving improper behavior around underaged boys. Perhaps it all stemmed from a traumatic period in his life when a trio of family members passed away. As he wrote in *My Story*, "Between the age of 15 and the time I left college during my senior year at the age of 21, I lost my mother, father and brother. Tennis, along with everything else in life, lost flavor and I tossed them all to the discard."

Be that as it may, Tilden accomplished mightily across his astonishing amateur career. He was victorious in 138 of the 192 tournaments he contested between 1912 and 1930, and only 26 times did he fail to at least reach the final round. His career winning percentage in matches was 93.6 as he finished with a mind boggling 907 match wins against only 62 losses.

No wonder he was so much larger than life. Making it all the more remarkable was how Tilden achieved celebrity status at a time when other athletes including baseball's Babe Ruth and boxing's Jack Dempsey were household names all over the United States.

Tilden was singularly influential in his sphere, most notably during his dominance deep into the 1920s. As the renowned American sportswriter Frank DeFord put it in his biography *Big Bill Tilden*, "No man ever bestrode his sport as did Tilden. In those years [1920–26] it was not just that he could not be beaten; it was nearly as if he had invented the sport he had conquered … Tilden simply was tennis in the public mind. Tilden and tennis, it was said, in that order."

Leaving the amateur game and transitioning to professional tennis meant that Tilden would no longer compete at the four majors. Although he was undeniably past his prime, Tilden remained formidable. At 37, his match-playing prowess and tactical acuity were still extraordinary. But the fact remained that he was facing much younger adversaries who were aware that Tilden was no longer as swift afoot and perhaps not as imposing with the weight of his shots.

Professional tennis was for the most part a wilderness for gigantic achievers like Tilden compared to what they had previously experienced in amateur tennis. The amateurs played frequently at plush clubs on their circuit, and always looked forward to showcasing their talent at the glamorous Grand Slam championships, particularly Wimbledon and the U.S. Championships in those days. The professionals were often relegated to cramped and dank arenas and were barred from those major events that had once been their bailiwick, but Tilden had already conquered that world comprehensively with his record seven U.S. along with three Wimbledon singles titles.

The amateur governing bodies in tennis were not above paying players "under the table", and over the decades, until "Open Tennis" arrived in the spring of 1968, this practice led to what became known as "shamateur" tennis. Sometimes players would stay in the amateur game and take the illicit money until they were ready to move on to other opportunities in the business world.

Tilden, however, was wedded to tennis in every way. It was his lifeblood. Without a racket in his right hand he would have felt lost and incomplete. At this stage of his career, he essentially had no alternative but to play professional tennis in relative obscurity and continue to define himself as an enduring champion in less appealing surroundings. He may have been in his late thirties,

Performing on municipal courts, Bill Tilden attracted an appreciative crowd in 1925.

but that did not mean he could not summon majestic tennis periodically.

In 1931, Tilden was victorious at the prestigious U.S. Pro Championships.

He easily secured the French Pro Championships in 1934, and was runner-up to countryman Ellsworth Vines at the London Indoor Pro Championships in 1935.

Meanwhile, he won some pro tour series decisively over Karel Kozeluh in 1931 and Hans Nusslein the following year. But age caught up with him again. The powerhouse Vines defeated Tilden in 47 of their 73 head-to-head contests on a 1934 tour. And in 1941 countryman Don Budge took Tilden apart in 47 of 53 matches. Tilden turned 48 that year.

Prideful but unwavering, Tilden plodded on. In 1945 he reached the semifinals of the U.S. Pro Championships at 52. At the U.S. Pro Hard Courts he was also a semifinalist that year, losing to Budge but beating Fred Perry in the third-place match. As late as 1951 he was a quarterfinalist at the U.S. Pro Championships. Two years later, Tilden was ready to leave his California home to compete in Cleveland at the U.S. Pro Championships when he passed away at the age of 60.

Tennis, unmistakably, had been his life. His entire life. His sole identity. The 6'2" Tilden altered the trajectory of the sport as much or perhaps more than any player has ever done. He may well be the immortal of all immortals in American tennis history.

Wills Moody was a stalwart backcourt practitioner because she weighed the percentages so impeccably.

HELEN WILLS MOODY

Full name	Helen Newington Wills Moody
Birthdate	6 October 1905; died 1 January 1998
Place of birth	Centerville, California
Major singles titles	8 Wimbledon (1927–30, 1932–33, 1935, 1938); 7 U.S. Championships (1923–25, 1927–29, 1931); 4 French Championships (1928–30, 1932)

While Tilden was ruling the universe of men's tennis in the 1920s and on into the thirties – reshaping the sport in a multitude of ways with the force of his personality and the diversity of his game – the first female superstar tennis player from the United States was stamping her authority on the landscape of the sport with similar force, impact, and persuasion.

Helen Wills Moody came from the west coast, growing up playing on the hard courts of California, establishing herself as an impenetrable figure with an utterly calm disposition that was the polar opposite of Tilden's theatrical demeanor. She was supremely disciplined and determined, ruthless in pursuit of her highest aims, and ever dignified and unruffled on the court. Hence, Wills Moody was given the nickname "Little Miss Poker Face" because she held her emotions in check and refused to allow opponents to see any sign of weakness or vulnerability.

Wills Moody's ledger was so impressive from the early 1920s until the late 1930s that she established herself indisputably as the finest American woman player of the first half of the twentieth century. For nearly seven years, from 1927–33, she was unbeaten in singles. This remarkably ambitious woman collected no fewer than 19 major singles titles altogether, a figure surpassed only by Serena Williams among American female players.

Revered in her field as an implacable competitor and perfectionist who left no stone unturned and operated purposefully and almost unerringly from the backcourt, Wills Moody would not tolerate self-inflicted wounds.

Wills Moody was better known for her incomparable groundstrokes but her serve was underrated.

She was a masterful percentage player with surgically precise strokes who seldom made mistakes. Her strategy revolved around finding patterns that made her adversaries uncomfortable. An extraordinarily big hitter for her time, Wills Moody measured every shot exceedingly well, displayed masterful ball control off both sides and blended power and accuracy unassailably.

This American original was largely an introvert who deliberately kept her distance from the other players away from the arena, but her self-assurance on the court rattled opponents who saw no sign of weakness from the imperious Californian. What they witnessed instead was an imperturbable champion who presented herself as untouchable in the battlefield of competition – and was more than prepared to back up that perception with triumphs born of acute self-awareness and uncanny court sense.

Winning became a habit early. She was groomed to make precision the hallmark of her game. When she was 14, Wills joined the Berkeley Tennis Club near her California home. One of her guiding forces, William "Pop" Fuller would put handkerchiefs in the corners of the court as targets for Helen to hit, which contributed tremendously to her deadly accuracy from the baseline. At 15 and 16, she captured the National Girls' 18s Championships in 1921 and

1922, and those victories led her into the wider world of women's tennis. Wills headed east to the fabled West Side Tennis Club in New York and took her first major title on the lawns at Forest Hills, claiming the crown at the 1923 U.S. National Championships.

Surviving a tense encounter with Great Britain's fleet-footed Kitty McKane 2-6, 6-2, 7-5 in the quarterfinals, Wills Moody went on to rout the Norwegian Molla Mallory 6-2, 6-1 in the final. Mallory had won that prestigious tournament seven of the previous eight years, but the 17-year-old American was unstoppable. She performed with a maturity well beyond her tender years.

As Wills Moody wrote in her autobiography, *Fifteen Thirty*, about that landmark moment in her tennis evolution: "Had anyone told me that I was to be champion of the United States, I would have thought that I would be so full of joy that life itself would be painful to live. Now that I had actually won, things didn't feel differently at all. I was delighted and happy, of course, but the universe had not changed."

That was not an entirely accurate assessment. The universe of women's tennis would never be the same. Wills had altered that world irrevocably and she would remain in the forefront of the sport until late in the following decade. On so many levels, the American women's game and, for that matter international tennis, were permanently altered by a teenager of a rare ilk who played a brand of tennis designed to impose her own assertive game while systematically breaking down her opponents.

Although the ensuing years would find Wills Moody exploring other endeavors, including attending the University of California where she studied art and earned a Phi Betta Kappa key, painting and newspaper reporting, tennis was her primary mission. Nonetheless, she approached everything she did with purpose, pride, and unrelenting determination. Her artwork was displayed prominently at a London gallery in 1929. When she was not physically fit to play Wimbledon in 1934, she reported on the tournament for the London *Daily Mail* and put in long hours to do that job properly. The year after she retired, Wills Moody published a novel entitled *Death Serves an Ace*.

Prior to the arrival of Wills Moody, there had been a number of prominent American female players, including one of her mentors Hazel Hotchkiss Wightman (a four-time U.S. Champion), May Sutton, and Mary K. Browne; however, none of these players were cut out to scale the heights the way Wills Moody would.

Across the 16-year stretch from 1923–38, Wills Moody was so imposing and indestructible when she was free from injuries and eager to put herself on the line, she had but one true rival. Only the charismatic Frenchwoman Suzanne Lenglen was on or above her level. Lenglen was as unbeatable as Wills Moody during her dominant days from 1919 to 1926, when these two superstars collided for the only time in their sterling careers. They met on 16 February 1926 when Wills was still in college and not quite at the peak of her powers. Lenglen, meanwhile, was moving just past her absolute prime.

Lenglen was victorious in this eagerly anticipated clash, toppling Wills 6-3, 8-6 on the clay courts in her native France. It is regarded as one of the most important tennis matches of all time because of the extraordinary stature of both players and the fact that they would never meet again. Lenglen left amateur tennis and played a brief pro tour against Mary K. Browne, while Wills Moody headed into the most prolific period of her career when no one could beat her from 1927 to 1933. They went their separate ways, but avid followers of the game were not rejoicing about that. Had they clashed regularly over a good many years, tennis would have celebrated a riveting series between the ballerina-like Lenglen and the majestic Wills Moody.

I interviewed Wills Moody over the telephone from my New York office at *World Tennis* magazine in 1986 on the 60th anniversary of the much-heralded Cannes skirmish she had with Lenglen. She was then 80 but her recollections of the duel with the Frenchwoman were vivid. She realized that this match was historically of the utmost significance but also was amused, retrospectively, that making the trip to France meant so much to her.

She told me, "The first thing I think about is my mother, who didn't want me to go. And my father didn't see much point in it. I just don't know why I thought it was the end of the world to leave the University of California to go to the south of France. I almost cried I wanted to go so much. I begged and begged, and looking back it doesn't make much sense at all."

Looking at that experience from the standpoint of her tennis education, Wills Moody said, "She [Lenglen] had more generalship on the court than I did. What I mean by that is that she had the game down to a pattern in her mind which was the best that she could possibly use according to her ability. I had more power and endurance."

Interestingly, Wills Moody added, "It was not a disappointment not to play Lenglen again. I was very young for my age then and I thought next time I will

Wills Moody at a 1929 exhibition of her sketches in London.

win. [But] I didn't care if there was a next time. Nothing ever bothered me."

She held to that philosophy across the board as a champion with a clear set of priorities and seldom if ever did she get in her own way. After that initial Grand Slam tournament victory at Forest Hills in 1923, Wills Moody came through almost automatically when it counted – and even when the stakes were not as high. She simply did not let her guard down, and playing bad or indifferent matches was out of the question.

There were years when she was troubled by a bad back and that kept her out of circulation, but her success rate was astounding. She won the U.S. Championships again in 1924, 1925, 1927, 1928, 1929 and 1931, securing seven singles titles in all. At Wimbledon, she was beaten by Kitty McKane 4-6, 6-4, 6-4 in the 1924 final after building a 4-1 second set lead. But she never lost again

A contemplative Wills Moody was always intense prior to big contests.

at the shrine of the sport, taking the title eight times between 1927 and 1938, winning 55 of 56 matches in total and her last 50 in a row. Not until Martina Navratilova was victorious in 1990 for the ninth time did anyone – man or woman – win Wimbledon more times in singles.

In those days of more restricted air travel, Wills Moody never made the

The numbers Wills Moody achieved speak loudly for the rarity of the standards she set.

trip "Down Under" for the Australian Championships, but she did claim the title on all four occasions (1928, 1929, 1930 and 1932) when she went to Paris and played on the red clay at the French Championships. The other outstanding American women players who established themselves as all-time greats – most notably Serena Williams, Chris Evert, Billie Jean King and Navratilova – played many more majors than Wills Moody did. Williams appeared in 81 Grand Slam tournaments, Navratilova played in 67, Evert 56, and King 51.

Wills Moody competed at only 22 "Big Four" events, but she won 19 and lost only three times – all in the final. She was competing for nearly two full decades, facing new waves of players, moving out of her teens, through her twenties and on into her thirties when her body was declining and her nerves were sometimes surfacing.

The numbers Wills Moody achieved speak loudly for the rarity of the standards she set. She captured over half of the tournaments she played in a career stretching from 1919–38, winning 52 of the 92 she played and securing 398 match victories against only 35 defeats for a 91.9 winning percentage. In that golden stretch between 1927 and 1933, she won 158 consecutive matches, 27 tournaments in a row and the bulk of her majors.

She defined herself at every stage of her career as a champion of the highest order. But it was in the latter stages of her career that she displayed her character most commendably. Two matches from her final years are illustrative of the steely resolve and immense poise of Wills Moody on the premier stages of the sport.

In the 1935 Wimbledon final, Wills Moody took on Helen Jacobs. Hailing from Arizona, Jacobs was a consummate match player, taking the title at Forest Hills four years in a row from 1932–35. In the 1933 final at Forest Hills, she had toppled Wills Moody for the first time, but that triumph was somewhat diminished when Wills Moody, suffering from severe back pain, retired at 0-3 in the third set of the final-round duel.

On the British lawns less than two years later, Jacobs seemed poised to upend Wills Moody with a full-fledged victory in the final. The two Americans had fought ferociously through an arduous afternoon on the famed Centre Court, and on this occasion it was Jacobs who seemed to have the upper hand and the sounder game. She played one of the finest matches of her career while Wills Moody was slightly subpar.

Author Larry Engelmann released a widely acclaimed book in 1988 called *The Goddess and the American Girl* about Lenglen and Wills Moody. Explaining how Wills Moody took 18 months off from 1933 into 1935 to rest from her injuries, Engelmann wrote, "There were limitations now. She had lost a step or two and she would never again be as fast. Now she had to think more and anticipate shots more accurately. She had to use her head. She had to plan and to watch and to calculate more carefully. Finesse was now the name of the game. She had to save the big weapon, the booming forehand winners. She had to outsmart her competitors on every shot."

Jacobs was a seasoned competitor who knew full well that the Wills Moody of this period was no longer the towering player she had once been. Jacobs was dressed in her familiar comfortable shorts while Wills Moody wore her usual knee length skirt. After they split the first two sets, Jacobs took a 5-2 lead in the third set of this absorbing final, but Wills Moody was not going to surrender, not even with her back to the wall.

Wills Moody seemed fatigued when she lost the second set and fell behind so precariously in the third. At 5-3 Jacobs advanced to match point. She came to the net and Wills could only throw up a desperate lob. But the lob was not that high, so Jacobs elected to take it on the bounce rather than out of the air. She went for the overhead but her shot hit the net tape and fell back on her own side of the net.

Wills Moody had survived a serious crisis, and her resilience from there on was remarkable. On a run of five consecutive games from the brink of defeat, she rallied valiantly to beat a despondent Jacobs 6-3, 3-6, 7-5. She had always been a big-occasion player who usually succeeded in straight set finals, but this time she had been forced to reach back with all of her resources to salvage a victory that seemed highly unlikely. In fact, even she could not quite believe that she had won that final when she walked off the court. She asked a friend to confirm that victory was a reality and not a dream.

Three years later, Wills Moody played the final tournament of her spectacular career on the British lawns and won her last of eight titles. That was no mean feat. She was 32 but time had taken its toll and Wills Moody was well aware that she had very little left in her competitive arsenal. In taking that 1938 Wimbledon title, it was as if she was destined to succeed and was being rewarded for a lifetime of dedication. Well past her prime, she fashioned success largely on inspiration and memory. She was seeded

No.1 based on the fact that she had only lost once in eight previous appearances at the All England Club, but by no means was Wills Moody the clear favorite.

And yet, despite a number of less than stellar performances in the earlier rounds, the 5'7" Wills Moody marched through the draw methodically without conceding a set. Tennis fans were yearning for her to meet the No. 2 seed and swiftly emerging American Alice Marble in the final but Jacobs prevented that from happening by defeating Marble in straight sets. Marble might well have given Wills Moody more than she could handle had they played, but it was not in the cards.

And so Wills Moody confronted Jacobs for the last time. The score was locked at 4-4 in the first set. Jacobs had her right ankle bandaged and still was holding her own. But in the ninth game she jumped while trying to make a high backhand volley and her landing was uneven. Jacobs had torn her Achilles tendon and thereafter her mobility was severely impaired. Wills Moody surged to a 6-4, 6-0 triumph.

She had concluded her astonishing career at the Grand Slam tournaments precisely as she had hoped she would, victorious in the last major she would ever play. A few weeks later she was victorious at the Irish

Wills Moody displayed impeccable technique.

Lawn Tennis Championships, and concluded her career on that note.

Wills Moody's multitude of triumphs on the court was balanced in the larger game of life by some misfortunes. She met Fred Moody right after her loss to Lenglen in 1926. They married in 1929 and were divorced eight years later. Two years later she married polo player Aiden Roark, but their union ended in the early 1970s.

Helen Wills Moody was a transcendent tennis figure of such stature that the renowned Mexican artist Diego Rivera once did a painting of her. She is right up there among the most significant American athletes of all time. As Engelmann wrote in *The Goddess and the American Girl*, "Her adventure seemed, indeed, a reaffirmation of American ideals … She was an athlete, a great athlete. And she was beautiful, far more beautiful than most film stars. Celebrating Helen Wills, Americans celebrated tomorrow – a tomorrow of American ascendancy, of aesthetic beauty, of intelligence, of modesty, of romance and of optimism."

Budge on his way to toppling the formidable Gottfried von Cramm in the 1937 Wimbledon final, only weeks before defeating von Cramm again in a famous five-set showdown at the same site, dramatically lifting the Americans past Germany in the Davis Cup.

Don Budge

Full name	John Donald Budge
Birthdate	13 June 1915; died 26 January 2000
Place of birth	Oakland, California
Major singles titles	2 Wimbledon (1937–38); 2 U.S. Championships (1937–38); Australian Championships (1938); French Championships (1938)

No one in the history of American tennis was more revered by fellow players and fans alike than the redoubtable Don Budge, an exemplary all-court player with a highly effective serve, a formidable forehand, and arguably the greatest backhand tennis has ever seen.

He seemed born to achieve prominence on the biggest international stages, to represent his country honorably wherever he went, and to play the game entirely on his own terms with an unmistakable style, elegance, grace, and purity that elevated him immensely in the eyes of an appreciative public. He was known as the great J. Donald Budge to the public but was nicknamed "J. Donald God" by tennis insiders.

Budge was one of the mightiest of American competitors, but also a champion determined to leave a lasting legacy, to be cherished long after he retired. By the time he passed away at the age of 84, after a lifetime of chasing and realizing most of his largest dreams, Budge knew he had lived up to his highest ideals and performed splendidly when it counted.

He was a towering champion with a wide range of successes and unshakeable self-belief, but what set him apart along the ladder of history was the seminal season of 1938. That year he became the first player ever to win all four major championships in a calendar year for a highly coveted Grand Slam

Budge commenced that campaign at the Australian Championships in January, secured the French Championships in June, won Wimbledon in July and completed his magnificent journey through the Grand Slams with a triumph at the U.S. Championships in September. Only one player had come close to that milestone before Budge, and that was five years earlier when the Australian Jack Crawford took the first three majors and made it to the final of the fourth before falling narrowly short.

Budge wanted to make history. He could have left amateur tennis after a dazzling 1937 season, which featured victories in the last two majors of the season at Wimbledon and Forest Hills – as well as leading the United States to victory in the international team competition known as the Davis Cup.

But he wanted to propel himself into another realm of the sport by sweeping all of the majors. And so he did just that with a glorious run.

At first glance, Budge's almost seamless march through the four most prestigious tournaments was straightforward and uncomplicated, but that was not actually the case. In Adelaide, he dropped only one set in five matches. In Paris, Budge conceded three sets in six matches and then in the last two legs of that Grand Slam journey he lost only one more set in 13 matches.

And yet, those numbers told only part of the story. Budge had serious issues with his health until the U.S. Championships in New York, and that made him apprehensive.

In 1998, on the 60th anniversary of Budge's landmark Grand Slam, two years before he passed away, I spoke with him for a piece I was writing for *Tennis Week* magazine. He clarified what he had endured over the course of that season.

Budge told me, "That year was the era of the worst health for me. I lost my voice in the finals of the Australian Championships. Then I had diarrhea during the whole French Championships in Paris and I had to have sandwiches brought to the court during my matches. At Wimbledon I lost my voice again. Not long before the U.S. Nationals at Forest Hills I went to a dentist in New York. He took x-rays and discovered I had an abscessed tooth which had been bugging my whole system. He gave me a shot of penicillin, yanked the tooth and at Forest Hills I was stronger again. I was lucky as hell to get through that whole year doing that well, not knowing I needed to get that poison tooth out of my body."

Remarkably, Budge was at his very best in the four finals he played at those 1938 majors. The great players

Leaping for a backhand volley at Wimbledon in 1937, Budge soared to his first of six straight major titles.

The majestic Budge backhand in full flight.

rise to the biggest occasions, and Budge was no exception to that rule.

As he said in our 1998 discussion, "The final at Forest Hills with [my doubles partner] Gene Mako was the only one of the four that lasted over an hour. I beat John Bromwich in a 57-minute Australian final, defeated Roderich Menzel in 58 minutes in the French final, and although rain delayed my final with Bunny Austin of Great Britain at Wimbledon, the playing time was again under an hour. Mako was playing very well at the time and he knew my game well so that U.S. Championships final lasted longer and was more of a test, but I won in four sets."

Had Budge left amateur tennis behind him and accepted lucrative offers from promoters of up to $50,000 to turn professional, he would not have achieved such exalted historical status. "Little Bill" Johnston – Tilden's old rival – made his case for Budge to move on to the pro game. Johnston worried that Budge would not only be risking financial security by staying in amateur tennis but also put himself in peril by perhaps getting injured.

Although Johnston had Budge's best interests at heart, Budge followed his own instincts, and the triumphant Grand Slam quest was his vindication. As he explained it to me, "It was damned nice of Billy to give me his advice but I told him I was going to take a chance and try to become the first to win the four major championships in one year. No one had ever done it so I felt I would be worth more to any promoter if I did win the Grand Slam."

Budge was correct. Upon completion of his 1938 season, he signed a pro contract for approximately twice what he would have received had he made that move prior to securing the Grand Slam. And, by remaining amateur for one more year, he had amassed a record six Grand Slam championships in a row.

And yet, if the Grand Slam journey defined Budge more comprehensively than anything else he did, close behind it was a match he won when representing the United States in the Davis Cup against Germany's elegant Baron Gottfried von Cramm. They collided in the summer of 1937 in the Interzone finals held at a neutral site, which was none other than the All England Club at Wimbledon.

Only a few weeks earlier in the final of Wimbledon, Budge had taken apart Von Cramm in three straight sets. But now, with the U.S. and Germany locked at 2-2 in a five-match series, it would all come down to these two magnificent players battling ferociously to carry their country to an illustrious victory. The stakes could hardly have been greater.

Significantly heightening the drama, intrigue, and importance of the occasion was an incident that took place just before the players walked on court for their historic appointment. Renowned tennis-dress designer Ted Tinling, serving as Chief of Protocol, was ushering the players from the locker room out to Centre Court. They were almost out of reach when someone came along and told Von Cramm he was wanted on the telephone.

Tinling did not want to delay the proceedings, but Von Cramm sensed it might be an important call, and he took it. Tinling and Budge could hear Von Cramm talking but did not know who was on the other end of the line. They learned from Von Cramm that it was Adolph Hitler calling to wish him luck. When I spoke with Budge about that conversation 50 years later, he swiftly recollected, "Hitler was apparently telling Cramm that they had had enough of the Americans winning everything in the Olympics over there. They were hoping – and Hitler was hoping – that Cramm would beat me and bring the Cup back to Germany."

Meanwhile, adding to the drama was the fact that Tilden was coaching the German squad, which was infuriating to observers of American tennis who had watched him lead the Americans to victory seven years in a row from 1920–26. Budge soon had his hands full with the stylish German shotmaker. Von Cramm prevailed in a pair of hard-fought sets before Budge retaliated to secure the next two. On they went to a fifth set, and Budge knew the German was virtually unbeatable under those circumstances.

Budge told me in 1987, "Von Cramm always said that any time he got anyone into a fifth set, he felt he had a 3-to-1 advantage over them because of his physical condition and because he had won so many five set matches without any losses."

When Von Cramm moved in front 4-1 in the fifth set, the American's plight appeared to be bleak. But Budge held his serve in the sixth game and then went on the attack, following all of his returns into the net, putting away his volleys unequivocally, breaking the German. Soon he was even at 4-4. At 6-6, he broke again and then served for the match in the 14th game. A gallant Von Cramm saved four match points but on the fifth Budge succeeded. Despite falling onto the grass court after he followed through on a forehand passing shot – and not being able to see whether his shot had landed in or out – Budge heard the roar of the crowd and got up off the ground to run and shake his adversary's hand.

As Budge recalled, Von Cramm told him, "Don, that was absolutely the finest match I have ever played in my life. I'm very happy that I have played it against you whom I like so much."

I asked Budge if he might have suffered any long-term psychological scars if he had lost that monumental meeting with Von Cramm. He replied, "I still think I would have won the Grand Slam the next year, but who knows? Maybe I wouldn't have. I just don't think that the loss of one match – even one as important as this – would have hurt me that much. If you took one point away and gave it to Cramm, he would have been the winner. So one point one way or the other isn't going to kill you. Once a match is over, it shouldn't cloud your career."

While the most enduring moments of Budge's sterling career were those he celebrated in the spectacular 1937 and 1938 seasons – 14 tournament wins in a row, 92 straight matches, and six consecutive majors to establish himself as the king of amateur tennis – he went on to other notable successes in pro tennis starting with a stirring rookie 1939 campaign. As Budge explained in his autobiography, *A Tennis Memoir,* "I turned pro because, in a competitive sense, I was forced to. I simply ran out of fields to conquer in the amateur ranks. Another factor that hurried us all to the pros was

Don Budge, left, in 1939 with older brother Lloyd after a family match.

a common proclivity for dressing well and putting some money in the bank."

He would make more than $100,000 that year, which was a considerable sum in those days (about two million dollars in today's money). Budge defeated fellow American Ellsworth Vines 21-18 in a riveting 1939 head-to-head tour across the United States. That was no mean feat. Vines had been the sport's dominant force at the start of the decade, taking the U.S. Championships in 1931 and prevailing at Wimbledon and the U.S. Championships the following year. He was a powerhouse both on serve and off the ground, pounding the forehand with astonishing velocity. But Budge's all-court prowess,

especially his standout backhand, were too much for his compatriot.

That same season, Budge got the better of his old amateur rival Fred Perry of Great Britain, 18 matches to 11. In 1941, Budge routed Tilden 47-6. Tilden was 48 and well past his prime, but fans still enjoyed watching him display glimpses of days gone by while appreciating the primetime skills of Budge. Still going strong in 1942, Budge was the dominant force on a round robin pro tour, winning 52 of 69 matches against the likes of countryman Bobby Riggs, who had been the top amateur in 1939, Perry, and Frank Kovacs.

Budge had taken pro tennis by storm over the four-year period from 1939–42. In addition to his overwhelming success in head-to-head tours against formidable rivals, Budge reaffirmed his supremacy with triumphs at influential tournaments. In 1940 and 1942, he was the champion at the U.S. Pro Championships. Budge crushed Riggs in the 1942 final. Meanwhile, in 1939 he eclipsed Vines to take the

Budge was comfortable and highly efficient at the net.

French Pro Championships. That same year, he came out on top in a round robin event at the London Pro Championships. And so he took all of the most significant prizes in pro tennis and established himself unassailably as the best player in the world once more.

When the 1942 season concluded with Budge joining the Army Air Force, he was 27 years old with several more golden years seemingly ahead of him. But he had left the game to serve his country in World War II and suffered a shoulder injury in 1943 which had lasting implications. He was never the same player again.

Upon returning to civilian life back in the U.S., Budge was the runner-up at the U.S. Pro Championships four times between 1946 and 1953, but lost thrice to Bobby Riggs and once to Pancho Gonzalez. He displayed more than flashes of his old brilliance in a five-set semifinal loss to Jack Kramer in that same tournament on the lawns of Forest Hills in 1948. He also gave the highly underrated Riggs a run for his money on their pro tour series in 1946 before losing 24 matches to 22.

But he was unable to summon the sustained greatness of his bygone days.

Budge was born and raised in Oakland, California. That upbringing enabled him to benefit from the warm weather and nearly year-round ability to play tennis outdoors. But during his youth he found a passion for other sports that enhanced his skills on the tennis court. Budge played baseball, basketball, and even a bit of football. Competing in those different games was proof of his remarkable athleticism.

He wrote in his memoir, "Baseball was my first love and was responsible for my success in tennis, particularly with the backhand … I am more or less ambidextrous … though I write with my right hand, there are many things I do better with my left. When I first started playing baseball, I began naturally as a left-handed hitter."

But he decided "because it felt right" to play tennis right-handed. As a young boy he hit the backhand with two-hands but, as he got bigger and stronger, switched seamlessly to one hand. Meanwhile, he played basketball until he had to give it up to devote himself more fully to tennis as he finished high school. But he believed that the athletic requirements in the two sports and the footwork were almost identical.

Across his youth, Budge was short and scrawny, but after turning 18 he grew almost six inches in one year.

That spurt up to 6'1½" was crucial in helping Budge scale the heights as a player and realize his potential, despite the fact that he remained thin at a maximum 155 pounds. At the end of his teens, Budge's revered coach Tom Stow changed his grip on the forehand to an eastern, which was the standard "shake hands" method of holding the racket in those days. Budge improved markedly, rising from No. 9 in 1934 to No. 2 in his country in 1935 at 20. By the following year, he was the best American player and narrowly lost a five-set epic against Perry in the final of the U.S. Championships. Thereafter, he was unshakable through those vintage years of 1937–42.

Budge's heroic 1938 Grand Slam secures his place in the realm of immortals. As of this writing, only one other man – the extraordinary Rod Laver of Australia – has ever realized that feat in nearly a century since Budge made it happen. He was immensely proud of that achievement. When we spoke at the baggage claim in New York's Kennedy Airport after returning from Wimbledon in 1982, Budge told me, "Some young players and fans seem to think that it was not that tough for me to win the Grand Slam and that a lot of people could pull it off. They seem to have this idea that it was no big deal. I always tell them if that was true, why have so few players managed to do it?"

Kramer looking to attack on his way to winning Wimbledon in 1947.

Jack Kramer

Full name	John Albert Kramer
Birthdate	1 August 1921; died 12 September 2009
Place of birth	Las Vegas, Nevada
Major singles titles	2 U.S. Championships (1946–47); Wimbledon (1947)

Looking back across the vast historical landscape
of tennis in the United States, the man who has
done more than anyone else to shape the sport
on a multitude of levels is Jack Kramer.

He established himself among the most formidable American players ever while comprehensively changing the way the game was played by those who followed in his footsteps while he was still an amateur in the 1940s. He turned professional and thoroughly dominated all of his rivals for five sterling years with a mastery of his craft that was unanswerable. He took over as the promoter of the pro tour later in the 1950s and signed up one leading player after another.

There was more. After doing so much to bring about "Open Tennis", which allowed amateurs and professionals to start competing against each other under the same tent starting in the spring of 1968, it was Kramer who played a crucial role in the structuring of an annual "Grand Prix" circuit commencing in 1970. Two years later, he was named the first Executive Director of the Association of Tennis Professionals (ATP), serving in that capacity for several productive years and displaying outstanding leadership at a time when it was sorely needed.

In his own way and on his own steadfast terms, Kramer was ubiquitous inside the corridors of the game. He was a principled power broker with clear convictions and deep aspirations, a charismatic individual who left no stone unturned in fighting for what he believed in, and the most multi-faceted

Showcasing his excellent forehand volley, Kramer conceded only 37 games across seven matches as he ruled at Wimbledon in 1947.

man tennis has ever known. An authentic "American Original", he knew himself well, understood how to bring out the best in others, and was indefatigable in standing up for what he believed in.

Although he was born in Las Vegas, Nevada, Kramer largely developed his game in Southern California as an only child. His family moved to San Bernardino, California, just west of Los Angeles, in 1934 when Kramer was approaching 13. His family moved back to Las Vegas for one year but returned to San Bernardino before relocating to Montebello, east of Los Angeles. His father, a senior engineer for Union Pacific Railroad, selected a tennis pro for Kramer named Dick Skeen after deciding to work in California rather than Vegas to give Jack a chance to chase his tennis dreams.

Jack Kramer was a respectable basketball player as a kid but gave up that sport to devote himself to tennis.

He came under the guidance of Perry T. Jones at the Los Angeles Tennis Club. Jones was the czar of tennis in Southern California and he made Kramer a junior member at the L.A. Tennis Club. Kramer progressed swiftly and soon won the National 15-and-under Championships.

He found another tutor who was instrumental in his transition to men's tennis. As he wrote in his 1979 memoir *The Game*, "The two things that turned me into a men's champion from a boys' champion were good competition and a club player named Cliff Roche. Specifically, Roche taught me the percentages in tennis."

Kramer elaborated, "Roche's first law of percentage tennis was to hold your serve … What set me apart, what couldn't be taught, was that I could follow a ball in from the baseline with my forehand … I learned to slice the forehand going forward and busted all the usual percentages."

Benefitting from Roche's outstanding tennis brain, Kramer put considerable work into the development of a sound attacking game and a second serve that would eventually become one of the finest in the history of tennis. By the time he was 19, Kramer had broken into the U.S. top ten at No. 6 in 1940. Three years later, he was No. 2 in the nation. Kramer spent the next two years serving in the Coast Guard during World War II, and then started producing the kind of attacking tennis he always dreamed about. It was a far cry from the way Tilden and Budge played the game. They built their styles around supremacy from the backcourt and sustained groundstroke depth, although Budge was very adept at getting to the net selectively and soundly executing his volleys.

Kramer was a different competitive animal altogether. He was the first great player to implement the serve-and-volley game unrelentingly. His methodology became known as "The Big Game" and very few adversaries could effectively combat his aggression. He came forward calculatingly, never abandoned his percentage tennis philosophy, and imposed himself comprehensively as no one had ever done before. Kramer was the ultimate aggressor who believed unequivocally that a great attacking player would always conquer the supreme defensive competitor.

Over the course of the 1946 and 1947 seasons, the 6'2" Kramer was nearly invincible, completing his amateur career in style, losing only three matches in that remarkable span, taking three of the four major championships he played, soaring majestically above and beyond his rivals. In 1946 at Forest Hills, only weeks after turning 25, he sealed his first Grand Slam singles crown, closing that campaign with victories over fellow Americans Don McNeill, Bob Falkenburg and Tom Brown. Kramer swept 15 of the last 18 games in a 9-7, 6-3, 6-0 final-round triumph after Brown served for the first set at 7-6. As Allison Danzig wrote in the *New York Times*, "Jack Kramer had his rendezvous with his manifest destiny yesterday. The 25-year-old Californian at last sits on the national tennis throne for which he was ticketed for his future occupancy from the time he first came east as a junior."

The following year, Kramer won Wimbledon, conceding only 37 games and one set across seven matches. The top-seeded Kramer obliterated Brown again in the final, stopping his countryman 6-1, 6-3, 6-2. It was an immaculate match from a fellow in complete control of his powers. He became the first man ever to prevail at the world's premier tennis tournament wearing shorts, simultaneously setting himself apart by conceding the fewest number of games of any men's champion in the history of the event.

Later that summer, Kramer successfully defended his U.S. Championships title at Forest Hills. In the penultimate round of that tournament, he avenged a loss at Wimbledon the previous year to the left-handed Czech player Jaroslav Drobny by coming through in four sets, and then rallied valiantly to defeat countryman

Frank Parker 4-6, 2-6, 6-1, 6-0 6-3 in a hard-fought final. Kramer seldom found himself in such a predicament in that dominant stretch of his career, but made an outstanding comeback.

Kramer signed a pro contract and started a tour against Bobby Riggs on 26 December 1947 at New York's famous Madison Square Garden. A blizzard engulfed the city that evening and nearly 26 inches of snow piled up on the pavements, but that did not deter 15,114 fans from showing up. Kramer was upended by the guileful Riggs that evening, but he would eventually gain the upper hand in their 1947–48 match series and came out on top 69-20 after pulling away inexorably to win 53 of the last 58 matches they contested.

In his book, Kramer gave Riggs credit for the completion of his commitment to come forward almost ceaselessly. He explained, "What I gave tennis was the big serve-and-volley percentage attack game, and it really dominated the game for the next quarter of a century … But do you know why I started playing this game? Because it was the only way I could beat Bobby Riggs."

Finding the right recipe to take apart the clever and cunning Riggs so decisively set Kramer on a path to years of domination on the pro tour. He was the ultimate craftsman of his time, and Kramer understood better than any of his rivals what it took to succeed in a demanding environment requiring incessant travel and immense discipline.

There was absolutely no stopping the hard-charging Kramer now. After moving across the United States and North America from one dingy arena to another accounting for Riggs night after night, month after month, Kramer took on the 1948–49 U.S. Championships victor Pancho Gonzalez in an eagerly anticipated series. Unlike Riggs, a cagey all-court competitor who relied predominantly on his groundstrokes, finesse, and strategic acumen, Gonzalez was cut from virtually the same cloth as Kramer. He had a magnificent serve-and-volley game.

But Gonzalez was nearly seven years younger than Kramer and could not match his rival's match-playing skills, or day-in and day-out professionalism. Kramer was simply better on the biggest points, and decidedly more stable as a competitor. He defeated his fellow American 96-27 in their 123-match series which commenced on 25 October 1949 at Madison Square Garden in front of 13,357 fans and stretched through 1950.

By the end of his amateur days, Kramer was already very professional in his approach to training.

Gonzalez was dubbed "Big Pancho" by his peers but it was "Little Pancho" Segura who confronted Kramer next on the pro tour. Segura was groomed in Ecuador and attended college in the U.S., winning three NCAA Championships in a row. He developed a magnificent two-handed forehand and his tactical acuity was extraordinary. Yet he could not contain Kramer in the fast

Kramer in 1950 with his band of professional players who toured 100 American cities. Left to right: Pauline Betz, Kramer, Gussie Moran, and Pancho Segura.

indoor conditions where they played most of their matches. Kramer stopped Segura 64-28 in their 1950–51 duels. And then he essentially wrapped up his pro playing career in 1953 against the disciplined and often-undervalued Frank Sedgman, surpassing the Australian 54-41 in his toughest of all head-to-head tours. Sedgman – who had concluded a sparkling amateur career in 1952 with triumphs at Wimbledon and the U.S. Championships – was at his zenith while Kramer had moved past his prime at 33.

But he had done more than enough to be considered one of the greatest players in the history of the game and a uniquely influential American competitor. In addition to his astounding record on those head-to-head pro series tours, Kramer also secured the U.S. Pro Championships title in 1948 and the London Pro Championships at Wembley the following year, toppling Riggs on both occasions. He was lauded among tennis observers and his fellow players for the depth and quality of his second serve, one of the finest forehand volleys of all time, and a match-playing temperament of the highest order.

Now he turned to promoting the professional tour, signing up the leading male players year after year, raising the standards as best he could out on the road. As he told me in a 1997 interview for *Tennis Week* magazine, "I was insistent that we should continually follow the more successful way golf was promoting itself, so I would try to get the best amateur player of each year to turn professional. And I think doing that sold the game tremendously in America. As a promoter I was able to bring the game to 85 to 95 cities outside of the big cities on an annual basis and bringing these great names to those places helped popularize the game throughout the country. Deep down, I feel that might have been the best thing I ever did for the sport."

Kramer hoped his plan as a promoter would make "Open Tennis" happen sooner rather than later. It took much longer than he would have liked, but the fact remained that Kramer, starting a few years before he stopped playing, poured his heart and soul into taking tennis to another level for more than a decade. It was a sometimes thankless task but he dealt graciously with the political ramifications he confronted in a complicated sport and kept at it. But, not wanting to be an impediment to the emergence of Open Tennis, he eventually removed himself from his promoter's post about five years before the dream turned to reality.

The early stages of the "Open Era" were critical for tennis in many ways as the sport exploded with popularity, and different entities and individuals looked to exploit their opportunities and desire to play prominent roles in the evolution of the game. Kramer was right at the center of it all in two capacities. With the help of his old friend and renowned teaching professional Vic Braden, he created the Grand Prix circuit in 1970.

Others including Lamar Hunt with his World Championship Tennis Circuit and George MacCall with his National Tennis League were searching for ways to bring the players under their domain, but Kramer was not in accord with their way of doing things. As he told me in 1997, "The Grand Prix was a necessary thing because MacCall and Hunt had bought up all the good players. If they were going to take these players out of the mainstream of the game and hold events where they were going to get money for it, that meant they were gradually going to weaken the structure of Davis Cup, Wimbledon, the U.S. Open and so forth. So the Grand Prix was a good idea. The concept was really about establishing the top 20 events and players receiving points in all of them, and holding our Grand Prix Masters at the end of the year for the leading players. The Grand

Prix established a real circuit around the world so that people following tennis could know it wasn't a rinky dink game."

Kramer's next venture was as the first Executive Director of the Association of Tennis Professionals (ATP). Kramer was 51 when he accepted that prestigious position and it was tailor made for him. No one knew the inner workings of the game the way Kramer did after decades of deep involvement. He had a golden name in his universe not only because of his exploits as a champion player, expert promoter, and a leader on other fronts, but also because his Wilson Jack Kramer Autograph wood racket was one of the bestselling frames from the 1950s until the late seventies.

He would write in *The Game*, "There's a lot of kids around who probably think I'm some kind of brand name, who don't have any idea that a kid named Jack Kramer carried a racket before he became one."

Be that as it may, Kramer was more than ready to serve the ATP as their leader, and soon he would face his first test in the role. About nine months after the organization was formed at the 1972 U.S. Open, he was thrown into the media spotlight when a large number of male players boycotted Wimbledon in defense of a player's right to choose his own destiny. One of their players was French Open finalist Niki Pilic of the former Yugoslavia, and he had been suspended by the International Tennis Federation (ITF) for refusing to play Davis Cup for his country. His home federation claimed he had made a commitment but Pilic insisted that was not the case.

Pilic's suspension meant he was not eligible to play at Wimbledon. Nearly 80 players elected to join the boycott including 13 of the original top 16 seeds, most notably the defending champion Stan Smith, 1970–71 champion John Newcombe, Arthur Ashe, and Ken Rosewall. Kramer and the players on the ATP board fought in vain to find a compromise but their efforts failed.

Many of those players were sharply criticized in the media, particularly by the British press. But the chief target of the journalists was Kramer. He was lambasted by many writers who seemed to ignore that Kramer was a progressive traditionalist who had no intention of harming the game's centerpiece tournament. Moreover, the big-name players who fervently supported the boycott were not acting selfishly either. The likes of Newcombe, Smith, and Ashe were missing out on a serious opportunity to enhance their historical stature and willing to stand their ground, but none of them were ridiculed as recklessly as Kramer. The British media's disdain for Kramer was fundamentally irrational.

At Wimbledon in 1971, Kramer, long one of the leading commentators, calls a match for the BBC.

But those who took a longer view and examined that boycott through a different lens lauded Kramer for a highly principled stand. He was aware of an old proclamation that what is popular is not always right, and what is right is not always popular. As he told me the last time we spoke in 2008 when I wrote a piece on him for tennischannel.com, "When we had that boycott, Wimbledon was caught in the middle. They elected to support the President of the ITF, and the ITF's position was that they controlled the players. It was a principle that the ATP had to stand up for. All I could do was be as honest as I could in telling everybody what we at the ATP were about, and why we were doing it. The tennis writers understood the issues but decided to support Wimbledon, so we got hit on the chin public-relations wise something awful. I took the brunt of it and it cost me my job with the BBC, which I felt I had done awfully well. But it was worth it. If it came up again, I would do it again. It showed something about my character."

Kramer lives on an island among the American immortals. His impact on the men's game was the most far reaching of them all, by a considerable margin. Kramer, in my view, was undoubtedly "The Man of the Twentieth Century" in tennis. I asked him in 2008, about a year before he passed away at 88, how he wanted to be remembered. He paused for a moment before responding, "I think I played the game as well as anybody played it, and in a way that tennis was meant to be played. I didn't use any gamesmanship whatsoever, and won on making the best shot at the right time to break serve. I am very proud of what I did on my pro tours as a player. I beat some awfully good players. And I am very pleased with what I did as a promoter, taking the game to places that never had a chance to see good tennis. I feel I contributed a lot to the sport in different ways."

A gratified Connolly holds the trophy after taking her first title at Wimbledon in 1952.

Maureen Connolly

Full name	Maureen Catherine Connolly
Birthdate	17 September 1934; died 21 June 1969
Place of birth	San Diego, California
Major singles titles	3 U.S. Championships (1951–53); 3 Wimbledon (1952–54); 2 French Championships (1953–54); Australian Championships (1953)

Fifteen years after Don Budge had become the first player ever to win all four major championships within a calendar year for an historic Grand Slam, another unshakable American came forward with a clear-mindedness, ruthlessness, and icy ferocity that was every bit as impressive, realizing that singular feat of seizing the four premier titles in succession without a hint of hesitation.

Maureen Connolly was another in a long line of Californians who altered the face of both American and international tennis irreversibly. She was forthright, thoroughly dedicated to her craft, strikingly composed, and a champion through and through.

In 1953, Connolly established herself as the first female ever to win a Grand Slam, and only the second player to step into that elite territory. She was only 19, but the way she conducted herself on the court made her seem like a much older and more seasoned individual. Opponents with vastly more experience often felt inferior when competing against the teenager. Young as she was, Connolly was ready to embrace the challenges and pressures of elite-level competition and turn her dreams into reality.

Connolly's journey through her Grand Slam year began at the Australian Championships on the grass courts of Melbourne. The field was relatively weak compared to the other majors, but Connolly refused to let her guard down. She conceded only 11 games across ten sets in five matches, defeating her countrywoman Julia Sampson 6-3, 6-2 in the January final. Retrospectively, there was no way Connolly was going to lose in that tournament.

That was not necessarily the case at Roland Garros when Connolly took the French Championships in June. She was in jeopardy against Susan Partridge Chatrier, an Englishwoman married to Frenchman Philipe Chatrier. (He later became President of the French and International Tennis Federations. The stadium at Roland-Garros would eventually be named after him).

Partridge Chatrier had nearly toppled Connolly at Wimbledon the previous year, and now she took the first set and led 2-0 in the second in Paris before Connolly won 12 of the last 14 games in a 3-6, 6-2, 6-2 victory. But that was the only set Connolly lost in five matches. She would claim the crown with a 6-2, 6-4 win over her countrywoman Doris Hart.

Halfway to the Grand Slam, Connolly allowed five opponents a combined total of eight games on her way to the Wimbledon final at the All England Club, but waiting for her there was none other than the accomplished Hart, who was seeded second behind Connolly. Hart had ruled at Wimbledon two years earlier, and she had also captured the 1949 Australian Championships, along with the French Championships in 1950 and 1952. She later was victorious at the 1954 and 1955 U.S. Championships. Altogether, in singles, doubles, and mixed doubles, the versatile Hart would be the victor at 35 Grand Slam Championships.

Against Connolly in an epic 1953 Wimbledon final, Hart played perhaps the best tennis of her singles career, pushing her unwavering adversary to the hilt, reaching deep to find a formula to beat an inspired adversary who was also at her zenith. Connolly simply played marginally better tennis on the biggest points, and won a pair of extraordinarily close sets 8-6, 7-5 to prevail in the best women's final at Wimbledon of that decade.

It gave her the third leg of the Grand Slam, and no victory in her entire career meant more to the 5'4", 120-pound dynamo. She wrote in her autobiography, *Forehand Drive*, "Doris played the greatest tennis of her career, and so did I … I won the match 8-6, 7-5 but the points tally tells a far more graphic story. One point separated us in the first set, one in the second set! This was the closest I ever came to my 'perfect game'."

What made Connolly particularly proud of that contest was the boldness both she and her adversary displayed with their shotmaking. They went for

Connolly's march through that draw was reminiscent of the way she had launched her campaign for the Grand Slam.

the lines, used every inch of the court, and pushed each other to the hilt.

I spoke with Hart in 2003 to get her perceptions on that monumental match, and, 50 years after it was played, she still recollected it vividly. She told me in a piece I wrote for *Tennis Week* magazine, "It doesn't happen often that you come off the court after losing a major final feeling like you have won. But I really felt like I had won because I knew deep down that match was the pinnacle of my tennis. We both peaked at the same time."

Having collected the first three majors of 1953, Connolly was absolutely determined to confirm her status as one of the greatest players in the history of the game by succeeding for the third year in a row when she went to New York for the U.S. Championships at the renowned West Side Tennis Club in Forest Hills.

Her march through that draw was reminiscent of the way she had launched her campaign for the Grand Slam at the Australian Championships about eight months earlier. Connolly was primed for the occasion and inspired

Connolly on Centre Court at Wimbledon in 1952.

to release her best tennis rather than be crippled by apprehension.

In six matches at the last hurdle of her country's championships where the grass courts in New York could produce the most capricious of bounces, Connolly was supremely disciplined, keeping her mind uncluttered, driving her groundstrokes with immaculate pace, consistency and depth, putting her match playing acumen fully on display. Connolly was regally efficient, dropping only 22 games in six sets, casting aside a still unpolished Althea Gibson 6-2, 6-3 in the quarterfinals, No. 3 seed Shirley Fry 6-1, 6-1 in the semifinals and the No. 2 seed Hart 6-2, 6-4 to complete her mission.

Shaking hands with her formidable rival Doris Hart after an epic final-round duel at Wimbledon, Connolly felt she had played the match of her life.

As Allison Danzig wrote in the *New York Times*, "In forty-three minutes, with her devastating speed and length off the ground … Connolly took the match 6-2, 6-4. Miss Hart, a finalist five times … resorted to every device, including changes of spin, length and pace … But Miss Connolly was implacably on to victory in one of her finest performances."

That Connolly was so self-assured as she took the last of her four consecutive majors in 1953 was a testament to her tenacity and composure. Her capacity to play her best under pressure at the U.S. Championships with so much history on the line was commendable.

By that time in her scintillating career, Connolly was able to compete with an equanimity that had not been evident in her swift rise to stardom. She grew up with a deep obsession for the sport she loved. Her parents divorced when Maureen was only four years old, and for a good many years she was estranged from her father.

As a child, Connolly took ballet lessons. Her mother was a pianist and wanted Maureen to pursue that path, but it did not happen. At nine, Connolly saw two men playing tennis and was enraptured. She vowed in her mind that she would become a tennis player.

Soon she started playing the sport. Connolly was almost ambidextrous and wrote left-handed but decided with the help of a local teaching pro named Wilbur Folsom to play tennis right-handed. At 10 years and six months, she started playing junior tournaments and made it to the final of her first tournament in the 13-and-under division, bursting into tears after a loss. As she wrote in *Forehand Drive*, "Tennis to me was, even then, much more than just a game."

When she was 12, Connolly met the highly regarded coach and teaching professional Eleanor "Teach" Tennant in Los Angeles while playing a junior event. Tennant had worked in the 1930s with Alice Marble, another American standout who won Wimbledon in 1939 and secured four U.S. Championships titles between 1936 and 1940. Tennant was highly charged, brilliant, charismatic, dogmatic, and neurotic. She was in her late forties when she met and began guiding the impressionable Connolly along her tennis journey.

Buoyed by Tennant and her single-mindedness, Connolly would travel from San Diego to Los Angeles to work uncompromisingly on her tennis with her dynamic tutor. In that initial period, Connolly took up tap dancing to enhance her tennis footwork. But the most crucial step she took in those formative years as a 12- and 13-year-old was a sharper focus on technique that was instrumental in her long-term advancement.

Connolly explained in *Forehand Drive* that she had been using too much slice on her shots, but Tennant "gave me the flat shot which is absolutely essential to good tennis. Different coaches have different methods but Teach used a highly effective, imaginary clock system. I stood in the backcourt and imagined I was in the center of a large clock dial, with twelve o'clock directly behind me. I started my forehand at twelve, hit at nine o'clock and followed through to six o'clock. The backhand was just the reverse. I developed sound strokes, a power game and later in my career, if a shot soured, Teach would bring me back to this basic bit of practice and straighten out the shot."

The gains from this player-coach union were immeasurable but, in the process of making tennis the extreme focal point of her life, Connolly lost a part of herself. As she moved into her teens and beyond, Connolly wanted to go out on dates and enjoy herself from time to time, but Tennant did not approve. "Teach believed everything in my life should be sublimated to tennis. She was the field officer, I the troops, and we went into action with deadly purpose and total concentration."

As the years passed and Connolly excelled in the juniors and then at women's tournaments, Tennant was overbearing, but Connolly was winning. She tried to play through and move past her conflicts, realizing that sacrifices were required to reach her goals.

And yet, Connolly was aware that something dangerous and potentially catastrophic was building up inside her. As she wrote in *Forehand Drive* about Tennant, "She had lighted the flame of hatred within me – a flame that was almost to destroy me, even as I fought my way up to the championship of the world. It was the fierce flame of hatred. I hated my opponents. This was no passing dislike, but a blazing, virulent, powerful and consuming hate. I believed I could not win without hatred. And win I must because I was afraid to lose. The fear I knew was the clutching kind you can almost taste and smell, and the specter of defeat was my shadow. So tragically this hate became the rule of my obsession to win."

Winning became her habit, and for a long while Tennant was the architect of Connolly's destiny. At 14, Connolly became the youngest ever to take the National Girls 18s Championships in 1949, a title she defended in 1950. That set the stage for larger accomplishments ahead.

After capturing her last major at Wimbledon in 1954, Connolly was exhilarated, but only weeks later a horseriding accident ended her career.

In 1951, Connolly was the victor at Forest Hills for the first time at 16, claiming the U.S. Championships title, establishing herself as the youngest ever to win the women's crown. Tennant deliberately stoked the fires within Connolly before her semifinal contest against the top-seeded Hart. Tennant told a friend of Connolly's that Hart had referred to her as a spoiled brat. Incensed, Connolly toppled her former heroine 6-4, 6-4. Playing through a drizzle, and a rain delay later, Connolly was driven to put Hart in her place and make her older adversary regret that comment.

As she wrote, "I played some of the greatest tennis of my career. I shot for the lines, made impossible returns, applied crushing pressure

Connolly playing an early round match at Wimbledon in 1954 where she won her ninth and last major title.

and forced my foe every second. No sane player would have taken the reckless gambles I did. I never hated anyone more in my life."

In the final, Connolly held back Shirley Fry 6-3, 1-6, 6-4 after the score was deadlocked at 4-4 in the final set.

While Connolly's performance was not as dazzling as what she released against Hart, it was abundant proof of her class and composure under duress. Her outlook was now one of unmistakable optimism, and "Little Mo" was brimming with confidence.

She picked up at the majors in 1952 where she had left off the previous season. Absent from the Australian and French Championships because she was still in school, Connolly made a spectacular debut at Wimbledon. She did, however, have a considerable scare along the way. Facing Susan Partridge Chatrier in the fourth round, Connolly found herself precariously close to defeat. Trailing 4-5, 15-30 in the third and final set, standing two points from defeat, down to a second serve, she won that crucial point. A fan who was in the U.S. Air Force screamed, "Give 'em hell, Mo!"

Connolly was deeply touched and spurred on by the young fellow's encouragement. She proceeded to lift her game decidedly, and rallied for a 6-3, 5-7, 7-5 triumph. Seeded second, she won that tournament, defeating No. 4 seed, three-time former champion and countrywoman Louise Brough 7-5, 6-3 in the final. At 17, she was the youngest woman to win Wimbledon since May Sutton in 1905. Connolly rescued herself after Brough served for the opening set at 5-4, and collected six of the last seven games from 0-2 in the second.

That was a landmark tournament for Connolly not simply because she took the title on her first attempt, but because she parted ways with Tennant. Connolly had torn a shoulder muscle shortly before Wimbledon and Tennant wanted her to pull out of the tournament. Connolly sharply disagreed. She had treatments for the ailing shoulder twice a day over the fortnight of Wimbledon. That deep disagreement permanently broke up what had been a strong if fragile relationship.

Later that summer, Connolly made it two in a row at Forest Hills, defending her title with aplomb. She was untroubled going into the semifinals, but in that round confronted a savvy Shirley Fry, nearly bowing out of the tournament. Fry broke up Connolly's rhythm by deliberately slowing down the speed of her shots. She took the first set and led 4-2 in the second, but Connolly came out of that crisis with the temerity that was almost second nature to her. Winning ten of the last 11 games, she triumphed over Fry 4-6, 6-4, 6-1. In the final, Connolly was ready for the superb court craft of Hart, overcoming her tenacious adversary 6-3, 7-5, demonstrating her superiority once more as a big match player down the stretch.

At the end of that year, Connolly formed a critical alliance with the Australian maestro Harry Hopman, a former player and future Davis Cup captain renowned for his unflagging work ethic and motivational skills. He took over as Connolly's coach and gave his charge a new lease on life. Connolly benefitted tremendously from his wisdom and appreciated the way Hopman understood that simplicity is the essence of perfection. Hence, with his emphasis on hard work, physical fitness, and sound strokes, Connolly was a happier player with a significantly altered outlook. Hopman had her running and skipping rope. He inspired Connolly and turned her into a better athlete and lower-key competitor.

As Connolly wrote in *Forehand Drive,* "I reached the pinnacle of my game because of him. Gradually under Hop's training I became so fit I could play all day. Hop became convinced that if I were on top of my game and in top physical condition I would be virtually unbeatable."

Hopman contributed mightily to Connolly winning the Grand Slam, and the following year their partnership started in the same winning mode. She extended her personal winning streak at the Grand Slam tournaments to nine in succession by capturing the French Championships and Wimbledon back to back in 1954 on the clay and the grass. At Roland-Garros, she was never seriously threatened, gliding to a second title in a row. At Wimbledon,

Connolly confronted Louise Brough again in the title-round, prevailing 6-2, 7-5 after trailing 2-5 in the second set. She said, "I became furious with myself – not Louise – and I knew it was time to unleash everything I had."

Connolly had the world of tennis at her feet, with many proclaiming that she was the best female player ever to lift a racket. A pro career seemed entirely possible, as did remaining an amateur and winning clusters of additional majors. But only a few weeks after Wimbledon, her career would be cut short due to a freak accident. On 20 July 1954, she was horseriding near her home. A cement mixer truck came around a blind corner and frightened her horse. Connolly was thrown to the ground and hit by the truck and her right leg was badly injured. Despite attempting a comeback the following year, she never competed again.

Connolly had married Norman Brinker, a U.S. Olympic equestrian, and they had two daughters. She offered advice to a number of players including Ann Haydon Jones of Great Britain, and did some tennis commentary at

Connolly walks off court with Doris Hart (left) after one of their many great battles.

Wimbledon. But, tragically, when she was only 34, Connolly lost her life to cancer.

She left behind a shining legacy. Connolly achieved prodigiously from the ages of 16 to 19, and through those four years she had no legitimate rival because for a brief and brilliant span she reigned supreme with the weight of her shots and superior footwork.

Connolly must be heralded as an American tennis heroine who took the women's game to a new level, an iconic figure who transcended the sport and inspired the sports fans of America with her boundless enthusiasm and heart of gold.

In 1949, having won the U.S. Championships for the second straight year,
Gonzalez signed a professional contract.

Pancho Gonzalez

Full name	Richard "Pancho" Alonzo Gonzalez
Birthdate	9 May 1928; died 3 July 1995
Place of birth	Los Angeles, California
Major singles titles	2 U.S. Championships (1948–49)

Perhaps no other American male or female tennis player has lasted longer in the hearts, minds, and imaginations of the sport's most fervent fans than the charismatic and enigmatic Pancho Gonzalez. From the late 1940s into the early 1970s, his prominence was extraordinary and his exploits astounding.

An explosive personality and immensely imposing figure prone to inexplicable and irrational outbursts on the court, Gonzalez would almost always emerge from dark mood swings to find sunlight in his psyche and turn likely losses into rousing victories. His ferocity left spectators dazzled and kept adversaries at bay.

Gonzalez climbed to the top of the American tennis mountain in 1948, reaching No. 1 in the United States when he was just 20. No fewer than 24 years later, only three months shy of 44 years old, Gonzalez claimed the last singles title of his career in Des Moines, Iowa. At the end of that year, he was ranked ninth in the United States, which was no mean feat. He was a fearless individual with a seemingly limitless supply of willpower; the bigger the stakes, the better he played. Gonzalez was as imposing a champion as tennis would ever produce.

He was a big man for his time, standing at 6'2" or 6'3" (depending on your source), weighing 180 pounds when he was in the best of shape. His eating habits were erratic but whenever Gonzalez reached a point where he felt his tennis was suffering

from being overweight – or out of shape due to dietary issues and his habit of smoking cigarettes – he took matters into his own hands. As Gonzalez told *Sports Illustrated* magazine during his heyday in the 1950s, "If I lose a few matches, I stop smoking, go to bed early and pay more attention to what I eat. In a few days I'm all right again."

Gonzalez was the first of seven children. His father, Manuel, was a house painter. His mother, Carmen, was a seamstress who gave Pancho his first tennis racket, which she bought for 51 cents as a Christmas present when he was 12. His parents came from Chihuahua, Mexico and settled on the south side of Los Angeles where they raised Pancho.

His real name was Richard, but the nickname, given to him by a friend, stuck. His childhood shaped his life in a number of ways. He was underprivileged with a strict upbringing. Given the nature of his personality and outlook, Gonzalez understandably wandered into trouble over his teens, including burglarizing houses at 15.

Once he became immersed in tennis and realized he had some exceptional ability, Gonzalez wanted to leave high school and devote himself comprehensively to tennis. He did not have the approval of his parents to make such an audacious move. His father told him to go to school, find work, or get out of the house. Briefly he left before his parents allowed him back into their home. Meanwhile, Perry T. Jones, the czar of tennis in Southern California, informed Gonzalez that if he did not return to school he would be suspended from all tournaments.

Gonzalez defiantly disobeyed that order. He left high school after two years and was kept out of tournaments for more than three years. Gonzalez went into the navy but left after a bad conduct discharge in 1947.

That proved to be a turning point in his life. Gonzalez was ultimately reinstated into tournaments and made inroads in the men's game across that season, rising to No. 17 in the United States. All along, the cornerstone of his game was his magnificent serve. His motion was exquisitely fluid and the incomparable power on that delivery seemed effortless because his mechanics were impeccable. He could count on that

serve endlessly all through his career, but he also was outstanding at the net and had a knack for making low returns of serve that he blocked skillfully, making it tricky for opponents to dig out difficult volleys. He had a tremendous overhead as well. His ground game was not his strong suit but he could, when necessary, out-steady opponents from the baseline.

In 1948, only eight American men were seeded at the U.S. Championships when the field assembled at Forest Hills, and Gonzalez was at the bottom of that list.

Nonetheless, he survived an arduous five-set skirmish against countryman Art Larsen before ousting the top-seeded American Frank Parker in a four-set quarterfinal. Next among the Gonzalez victims was No. 2 foreign seed Jaroslav Drobny of Czechoslovakia, a formidable left-hander. Gonzalez battled from behind to win that one 8-10, 11-9, 6-0, 6-3. And so the 20-year-old Californian was in the final against No. 5 foreign seed Eric Sturgess of South Africa. Undaunted by appearing in his first major final and standing one match away from becoming the champion of his country earlier than anyone expected, Gonzalez met that challenge honorably, casting aside his adversary 6-2, 6-3, 14-12.

Gonzalez, however, was not ready to embrace his exalted status. In fact, he fell into a slump. He would tell *Sports*

Illustrated, "I lost so many tournaments the next three months [after winning at Forest Hills in 1948] that they called me the cheese champion." Hence, his fellow players and writers started calling him "Gorgo" which was a shortened version of gorgonzola.

The letdown did not last long. Although he took his share of hard knocks in 1949, he came back to New York and was victorious once more at Forest Hills, demonstrating a command of his craft and mastery of his surroundings that was commendable. Gonzalez was seeded second among Americans behind Ted Schroeder. He overcame a tenacious Art Larsen in another five-set quarterfinal and then rallied to defeatNo. 5 seed Parker in a four-set confrontation.

That set the stage for a dramatic duel with Schroeder in the final. Schroeder had been his nemesis, beating Gonzalez at one stage in eight of their nine duels. He was a ferocious competitor who was known for the essential soundness of his game. Schroeder had won Wimbledon a few months earlier with a fortitude rarely surpassed on the lawns of London. Four of his seven matches at the shrine went to five sets but he refused to surrender. At Forest Hills, Schroeder had secured two more impressive five-set triumphs over the Australian Frank Sedgman and the American Billy Talbert.

Facing Gonzalez, the top-seeded American Schroeder nearly toppled his opponent. Schroeder was ahead two sets to love but Gonzalez needed to find a way to get back into the match. He had lost in the fourth round of Wimbledon and he knew that any chance he had to turn professional would depend entirely on finding a way past Schroeder in the single most consequential match of his amateur career.

The 21-year-old soared to another level in the third set and sustained his excellence in the fourth, allowing Schroeder only three games in those two sets combined. The fifth set was tighter and tougher but Gonzalez was the better man on the biggest points. From 4-4 he took two games in a row to complete a 16-18, 2-6, 6-1, 6-2, 6-4 win for one of the signature victories of his career. As Allison Danzig wrote in the *New York Times*, "Richard (Pancho) Gonzalez' reign as national amateur tennis champion was extended for a second year yesterday, and no holder of the crown has shown more perseverance in enduring and surmounting the barbs of adversity than did the 21-year-old from Los Angeles."

He did indeed accept an offer to turn professional in a highly anticipated head-to-head series across America against Kramer. The journalist S.L. Price

Gonzalez defeating Sweden's Ove Bengtson in the second round of Wimbledon in 1969 a few days after his epic victory over Charlie Pasarell.

reflected on the 1949–50 Gonzalez-Kramer duels in a 2002 piece for *Sports Illustrated* magazine: "For 123 nights the two men played on canvas stretched over wood in high-school gyms, armories, even at an opera house. Kramer won by a punishing margin of 96 matches to 27."

Kramer was the vastly superior match player at that time and he better understood the rigors of the pro tour: traveling from one city to the next in the U.S., day after day and night after night, with little sleep. He had been out

there in that environment since the end of 1947 when he clashed with Riggs, and the veteran thoroughly exploited his experience and professionalism.

Gonzalez, meanwhile, could not navigate the territory. Kramer's "Big Game" was quite similar to his fellow American's, but the gap widened as Kramer zeroed in on what it would take to get the upper hand in these serve-and-volley showdowns. Once he built an early lead in the series, he was ruthless, unrelenting, and masterful

In his twilight at the 1969 U.S. Open when he was 41, Gonzalez remained a force, reaching the fourth round as the No. 13 seed.

in getting across the finish line time after time. He was never complacent or self-satisfied. Gonzalez, however, was baffled, dazed, and demoralized.

Losing so badly lingered long in Gonzalez's mind. Not until 1954 did he get back in the main mix when he surpassed an over-the-hill Don Budge, Segura, and Sedgman on a tour. In 1955–56 when he took apart countryman Tony Trabert 74-27, he

was back in the forefront on the head-to-head tours where he needed to be. He did fare well in the most prestigious pro tournaments, winning three London Pro championships in a row at the Wembley arena, toppling Segura and Kramer in the last two of those finals, rescuing himself from two sets down in the latter against Kramer in another of his patented comebacks.

He also made it to the final of the 1951 and 1952 U.S. Pro Championships but was beaten in both cases by Segura. Be that as it may, after he was humiliated by Kramer in the vast majority of their clashes and right up until the end of 1954, Gonzalez lost his larger self and retreated. As S.L. Price explained, "Gonzalez diddled away his early prime as a player, spending most of his time racing hot rods, bowling, breeding dogs, stringing rackets at his soon-to-fail tennis shop in L.A.'s Exposition Park."

And yet, the Trabert pro tour skirmishes got him back on track. In 1957, he eclipsed the "Little Master" Ken Rosewall, overpowering the diminutive Australian who was such a pure shotmaker 50-26. The following year, he confronted another Aussie Lew Hoad, a player many of his peers believed was better than anybody who had ever played the game when he was at his best. The explosive Hoad took an 18-9 lead in that series but his back started giving him problems and Gonzalez took full advantage of his superior serve to eventually come out on top 51-36.

Now, at the age of 30, Gonzalez curtailed a lot of his activity in pro tennis. He kept winning in his sporadic appearances, securing his seventh and eighth titles at the U.S. Pro Championships in 1959 and 1961, losing to Rod Laver in the final of that tournament in 1964. He was also the runner-up to Rosewall at the French Pro Championships in 1961. But he was no longer playing as regularly.

There were more semi-wasted years. He abandoned pro tennis in 1962, and hardly played in 1963. He enjoyed success periodically from 1964–67, most prominently in his 1964 tournament triumph at the U.S. Professional indoors in White Plains, New York when he took his quarterfinal over Rod Laver 1-6, 6-3, 6-3, ousted Hoad 6-8, 6-4, 6-3 in the semifinals and upended Rosewall 5-7,

3-6, 10-8, 11-9, 8-6 for the title after being behind two service breaks in the fifth set. At 36, this was a staggering display.

As Gladys Heldman wrote in *World Tennis* magazine, "It was the greatest single display of tennis that New York, if not the world, has ever seen. Laver was brilliant on return of serve. Hoad was the perfect shotmaker, and Rosewall was the Little Master of the all-court game – but Pancho won. No one who saw Gonzalez on those three days will ever forget him."

When "Open Tennis" arrived in the spring of 1968, Gonzalez was nearing 40 but delighted to have the opportunity to compete against all of the best players – amateur and professional – in his twilight. He had been barred from the four major championships for nearly two decades but wanted to demonstrate emphatically to the public that he was one of the greatest players in the history of the game and a warrior as well.

At the first French Open in 1968, he gave the public a chance to see him not far away from where he had once been. In the quarterfinals, he beat the Australian Roy Emerson. Emerson was slightly past his prime at 31 but at that time he owned the most Grand Slam singles titles ever garnered in the men's game at 12. He was almost a decade younger than Gonzalez and a supremely fit champion, but the American was stronger down the stretch. Although

Gonzalez was beaten in the semifinals by Laver, he had made a serious statement with his triumph over Emerson.

A year later, he celebrated one of the golden moments in the late autumn of his career. Taking on Charlie Pasarell – the No. 1 ranked American in 1967 – in the first round of Wimbledon in 1969 he was infuriated after losing a marathon opening set 24-22 when told that play would continue in the fast-fading light. He lost the second set badly after yelling at the umpire, and was booed off the court when the match was halted with Pasarell in the lead two sets to love.

The next afternoon, the surly Gonzalez was replaced by a much more composed and dignified version of himself, and he made one of the most spectacular comebacks of his sterling career. Twice in the final set, he rallied from 0-40 and triple match point down on his serve. Altogether, he saved seven match points in the sunlight on the renowned Centre Court. Showered with applause from the afternoon audience, the revitalized Gonzalez startled Pasarell 22-24, 1-6, 16-14, 6-3, 11-9 in five hours and 12 minutes – then the longest recorded match ever on the Wimbledon lawns. He would lose to Arthur Ashe in the fourth round of that event, but the victory over Pasarell lingered a lot longer in the hearts and minds of an appreciative public.

Later that season, Gonzalez made a magical run at the Howard Hughes Open in Las Vegas, cutting down one leading player after another, including John Newcombe, Rosewall, Stan Smith and Ashe, to win the title. It was an insignificant tournament in the overall scheme of things, but knocking out that elite cast of four shining competitors was a stupendous achievement for Gonzalez at 41.

His late career heroics didn't end there. In January of 1970 at New York's Madison Square Garden, he stunned Laver in a five-set encounter only four months after Laver, 31, had completed his second Grand Slam not far away at Forest Hills. As if to underline that his New York win was not simply a case of good fortune on a great evening against a subpar opponent, Gonzalez went back to Las Vegas a few months later to defend his Howard Hughes Championships crown and, lo and behold, toppled Laver again in a four-set final. Temperatures were in the nineties Fahrenheit. Gonzalez was 42.

It seemed as if Gonzalez was determined to remind everyone that he was an iconic athlete who could still dazzle fans with his mastery of the game. He did that again in 1971 at 43 with one of his young protégés on the other side of the net. In the final of the Pacific Southwest Open in Los

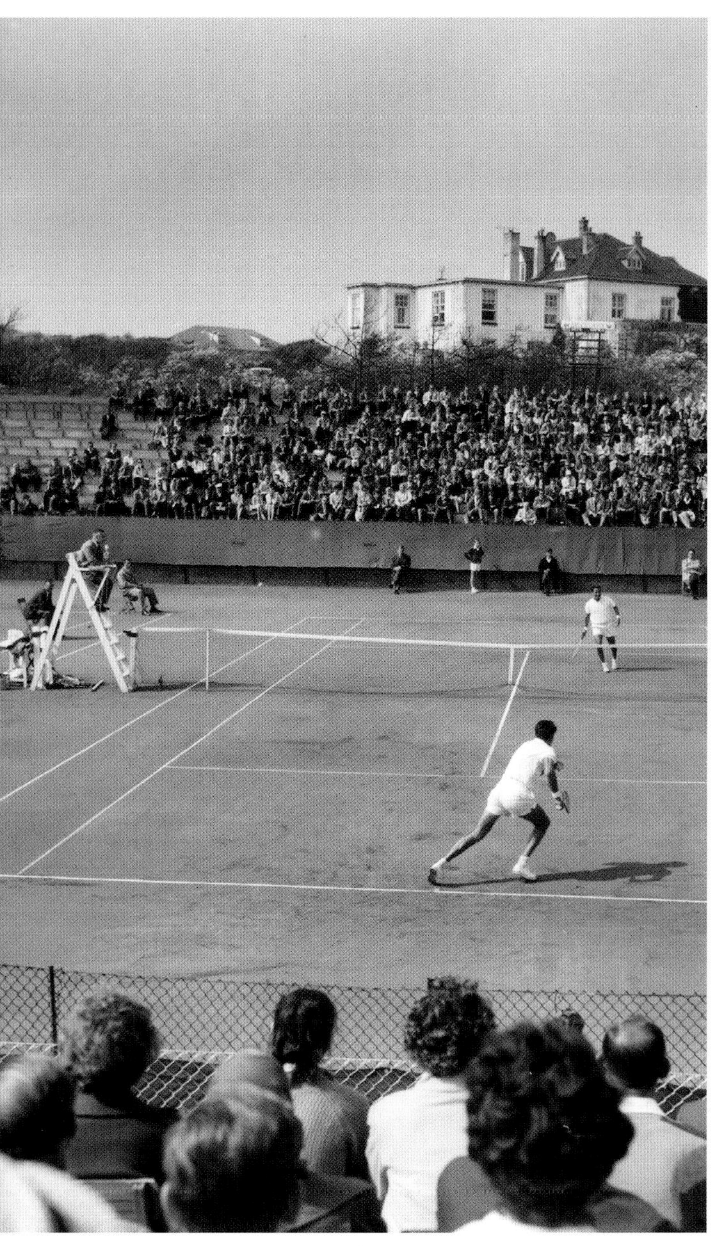

Pancho Gonzalez (bottom of photo) playing against Pancho Segura in 1961 on the pro tour.

Angeles, Gonzalez outmaneuvered 19-year-old Jimmy Connors from the backcourt and was victorious 3-6, 6-3, 6-3 in a crowd-pleasing spectacle.

After his playing career, Gonzalez moved on to other endeavors including television commentary. His last of six marriages was to Andre Agassi's sister, ending in divorce like all of the others. He had eight children altogether. He led a tumultuous life, bowing to cancer in 1995 at 67. He was a man of many sides, a conflicted individual, and a fellow who visited the extremes of his character across his entire lifetime.

How to define his legacy? He is one of the greatest and least appreciated champions of all time, as formidable a competitor as the game has yet seen, and a player with one of the two or three best serves in the history of men's tennis. He was a complicated individual who sometimes drowned in the sea of his own frailties, but his character was revealed on the opposite side of the ledger time and again with his capacity to find the best in himself when the stakes were highest. No American man in the history of the game has played top-level tennis for longer than did Pancho Gonzalez, but his inimitable and timeless talent has often been overlooked.

New York Times Pulitzer Prize-winning columnist Dave Anderson sums up the essence of Gonzalez's immortality better than anyone. He wrote in 2009 about this extraordinary figure, "He was the best tennis player not enough people saw."

In 1950, Althea Gibson became the first Black player to compete at the U.S. Championships, breaking the color barrier.

Althea Gibson

Full name	Althea Neale Gibson
Birthdate	25 August 1927; died 28 September 2003
Place of birth	Clarendon County, South Carolina
Major singles titles	2 Wimbledon (1957–58); 2 U.S. Championships (1957–58); French Championships (1956)

When Althea Gibson was controlling the climate of the women's game in the late 1950s, she overwhelmed adversaries with as big a serve as the women's game had yet seen, an intimidating overhead along with aggressive volleys off both sides, and a potency off the ground that was unanswerable.

From 1956–58, she collected five major singles titles, most notably capturing Wimbledon and the U.S. Championships in 1957–58. Only two women – Helen Wills Moody and Maureen Connolly – had been victorious in consecutive years at the two most prestigious tournaments in the sport.

But Gibson was not simply another great champion making the most of her opportunities. She was the first Black player – male or female – to claim the highest honors in tennis. Gibson was subjected to racial insults and slurs frequently across her spectacular career. She would show up at hotels across the U.S. where rooms had been booked in her name, and the proprietors would tell her they could not permit her to stay. She was often not allowed to eat in restaurants where her white colleagues were accepted.

Somehow, against all odds, Gibson kept pursuing her goals and realizing her dreams. She shied away from controversial remarks and almost unfailingly maintained her dignity despite being the

Gibson playing in Surbiton, England at the Surrey Championships in 1957. Weeks later she won Wimbledon for the first time in singles.

frequent victim of prejudice and harsh criticism at times by Black journalists and leaders who believed Gibson needed to be more outspoken.

Her childhood was, to say the least, arduous. Althea was the first of five children in her family. Born in 1927 in a small South Carolina town, she moved to Harlem when she was two. The days of her youth were nothing if not tumultuous. Her family had been

sharecroppers in South Carolina of cotton and corn before coming east.

Gibson's relationship with her father was an unhappy one. He would beat her from when she was very young. She ran away from home after one of those beatings and went to a police station. She would walk the streets of her city, avoiding going home sometimes for hours on end. She would sometimes ride the subway all evening long, go to friends' houses during the day and escape from the harsh realities of her life by going to the movies whenever possible. It was not unusual for her to skip school.

She once went to the Society for the Prevention of Cruelty to Children who took her in overnight before calling her parents the next morning. Her father proceeded to beat her again when she came home. Gibson then went to a shelter in New York and showed them the welts on her back resulting from her father belting her with a strap.

And yet, despite that nightmarish upbringing, Gibson found tennis. She had been impassioned about different sports, enjoying basketball among other games as long as she could remember. Initially she thought of tennis as a sissy sport but that impression would change radically once she was properly introduced to the game.

In her teens the New York City welfare department gave Gibson a place to live with her own room. She tried different jobs like working in a department store, which she preferred to going to school. The welfare department gave her an allowance while she was in between jobs. But, most importantly, Gibson started playing tennis remarkably well.

With the assistance of a collection from club members, Gibson joined the highly regarded Cosmopolitan Club not far from where she lived and started taking lessons on a regular basis in

1941 when she was 13. Soon enough, she caught the attention of two doctors from the south who were thoroughly devoted to the development of Black tennis players, Dr. Hubert Eaton and Dr. Robert Walter "Whirlwind" Johnson.

The two doctors had started tennis camps in their hometowns. Johnson lived in Lynchburg, Virginia while Eaton was located in Wilmington, North Carolina. Eaton was a former ATA (American Tennis Association) National 18-and-under champion. Johnson became the acknowledged "godfather" of Black tennis.

Johnson guided and mentored Black players at his home in Virginia. It was a mini-academy of sorts. He and Eaton were friends. Eaton, too, was a crucial figure at the ATA, which held tournaments for Black players who were not permitted to compete in USTA events with white competitors. He had a court at his home as well. The two doctors witnessed the 18-year-old Gibson competing at the ATA Nationals in 1945 and agreed she was enormously promising but sometimes haphazard in her play. They hosted Althea at their homes, dividing up the year with Althea living at Eaton's home through the school year while she resumed her education, and then spending the summers with Johnson. Gibson was encouraged to accept their offer by her friend, mentor, and boxing champion Sugar Ray Robinson.

Under the superb tutelage of Eaton and Johnson which started in 1947, she flourished. It was not simply that Johnson and Eaton could provide Althea with suitable competition and drive her to tournaments, but they shaped her character and taught her about decency and decorum.

Gibson was very tall for her era at 5'11", and swift afoot, powerful with surprising touch, and unswerving as a competitor. But her athleticism was unharnessed, her shot selection immature, her match-playing skills unpolished. That changed sweepingly over the coming years.

In the summer of 1947, she won her first of nine ATA National Women's Championships. It was a pivotal moment in her career.

As Sally H. Jacobs wrote in her 2022 biography *Althea*, "The victory marked a crucial juncture in her tennis career. Althea would go on to win the women's title every year for the next nine years, an unparalleled record that still stands today, making her the most dominant player in ATA history. Never again would she be beaten by a Black woman on the tennis court."

Gibson graduated from high school in 1949 and got a basketball scholarship to Florida Agricultural and Mechanical College in Tallahassee.

By 1950, boosted immeasurably by Eaton and Johnson, she was playing USLTA tournaments and reached the final of the U.S. Indoors. Her circle of boosters was doing everything in their power to get Gibson into the U.S. Championships at Forest Hills.

Eventually they succeeded, with a strong assist from the highly influential Alice Marble. Marble had won the U.S. Championships four times at the tail end of the 1930s, and her stature as a top-of-the line champion was indisputable. She wrote an editorial in *American Lawn Tennis* magazine strongly advocating for Gibson to be allowed to play at Forest Hills. Marble pointed out, "If she is refused a chance to succeed or fail, then there is an ineradicable mark against a game to which I have devoted most of my life … She is not being judged by the yardstick of ability but by the fact that her pigmentation is somewhat different."

The campaign for Gibson was a success. In a major breakthrough for her race, she was indeed placed into the draw at the U.S. Championships, but collided in the second round with countrywoman Louise Brough, the well-rounded player who had won Wimbledon three years in a row as well as the U.S. Championships in 1947.

Brough picked Gibson apart in the first set before Althea battled back to take the second. With the skies darkening

Gibson in 1956 captured her first major singles title and set the stage for the two biggest years of her career.

Gibson displaying her considerable skills at the net in 1956.

and a storm brewing, Brough moved to
3-0 in the third set but Gibson stayed
on the attack and went ahead 7-6
before thunder and lightning caused
a one-day postponement. When they
resumed, Brough claimed three games
in a row to prevail 6-1, 3-6, 9-7.

It was a painful defeat for Gibson,
but the fact remained that in a larger
sense she had won. As Jacobs wrote,
"Althea, who was just four days shy of her
23rd birthday, had brought down one
of the major barriers to Black athletes
in American sports, forever inscribing
in the record books her role as a racial
pioneer, whether she liked it or not."

Truthfully, Gibson did not necessarily
like to be examined through that lens.

But she did enjoy gaining experience as a more prominent player striving for excellence. Facing someone of Brough's caliber at her first Grand Slam championship and making it so close was a critical step in her evolution.

Some authorities were anticipating a speedy ascent from Gibson after her duel with Brough, but that was not the case. She still had a lot to learn about the game and her own skills.

Gibson returned to college that fall of 1950 and balanced her studies with her tennis, getting mixed results. In June of 1951 she made her debut at Wimbledon, becoming the first African American to compete at the shrine. Benefactors jumped in to help her financially with that trip, including heavyweight boxing champion Joe Louis, who paid for her round-trip plane ticket.

Gibson bowed out in the third round at the All England Club and then was routinely dismissed by Connolly at Forest Hills a few months later, also in the third round. She was ranked No. 11 in the United States at the end of that year. In 1952 she advanced to No. 9 in the U.S. rankings, and then No. 7 in 1953, when she graduated from college.

The next few years were mediocre for Gibson, although she made a significant grip change on her forehand from the continental to the eastern, which provided more control and power.

But then Gibson's tennis journey and indeed her life were altered irrevocably. She had been considering going into the army, but instead accepted a 1955 offer to go on an overseas tennis tour organized by the U.S. State Department.

In November of that year, she flew out of New York and headed to places like Sri Lanka, India, and Pakistan. After that tour she went on to win many tournaments, taking 13 of 17 that she played at one stage. Brimming with confidence, she captured her first major singles title at the 1956 French Championships with a final-round victory over the stylish Angela Mortimer, a player who had beaten her four times in the preceding months. A good many experts thought the No. 4 seed Gibson was ready to win Wimbledon, but, overcome by anxiety, she lost to Ohio-born Shirley Fry in the quarterfinals. Back in New York for the U.S. Championships, Gibson was beaten in the final by the master strategist Fry again.

But that 1956 season altered her outlook decidedly. She was now officially

No. 2 in the United States behind Fry and, by consensus, the second-best player in the world as well. Gibson herself, her growing legion of boosters and the tennis cognoscenti were all in accord that she was on the cusp of controlling women's tennis.

By 1957 Gibson was indeed ready to reach out and seize the mantle of supremacy in her sport. This was her time to shine the light on her athletic gifts, unbridled talent, and shotmaking explosiveness. The essential Althea Gibson gloriously emerged.

At Wimbledon in 1957, Gibson was the top-seeded woman and the favorite to secure the title. She did just that, taking six matches in a row without the loss of a set, conceding only 30 games, demonstrating that the fast-paced grass courts suited her aggressive game to the hilt. Alice Marble believed Gibson possessed the finest serve-forehand power combination in tennis, but she also was awfully tough to pass at the net. In the final, Gibson defeated her doubles partner Darlene Hard of California 6-3, 6-2.

Gibson and Hard had won four tournaments together, but in singles Hard had no answer to the weight and scope of Gibson's game.

As Fred Tupper wrote in the *New York Times*, "Althea Gibson fulfilled her destiny at Wimbledon today and became the first member of her race to rule the world of tennis." He added,

"The ladies took the stage amid a sea of waving programs as the temperature touched 96 degrees [Fahrenheit] in the shade. Miss Gibson was in rare form. Behind her serves and her severe ground shots, Althea moved tigerishly to the net to cut away her volleys."

With tennis's premier prize in hand, Gibson turned her attention to prevailing for the first time at her country's Grand Slam championship. With the same self-assurance and controlled aggression she had displayed in Great Britain, Gibson was the class of the field once more in New York, allowing her six opponents a total of 25 games and zero sets, finishing her sparkling run at Forest Hills with a comprehensive 6-3, 6-2 victory over the No. 2 seed Brough to become the winner at the U.S. Championships.

Allison Danzig wrote in the *New York Times*, "Althea Gibson wrote the second red-letter entry for the archives. The first Negro [Black] player to win the crown of tennis crowns at Wimbledon, in July, she became the first also to carry off our national women's grass court title."

The pattern was repeated in 1958 as Gibson strengthened her hold as the finest female tennis player in the world. At Wimbledon, she dropped one set in the quarterfinals, but the top seed completed her triumph in style, taking apart the British left-hander Ann Haydon Jones (who took the title 11 years later)

Gibson proudly displays her Wimbledon singles trophy in 1958

in a 6-2, 6-0 semifinal recorded in 40 minutes, and then upending Mortimer 8-6, 6-2 after rallying from set point down.

Gibson may not have felt invincible, but nonetheless her self-conviction was unmistakable. Back to defend her crown at Forest Hills, she did not falter despite battling a virus. In the final, she dropped her only set of the tournament at the U.S. Championships but battled back fiercely to topple Hard 3-6, 6-1, 6-2, making a remarkable number of excellent lobs in the final set when her countrywoman was trying to take the net away from her. For two years in a row, no one had been able to deny Gibson the game's twin-highest honors. Connolly had been

Gibson is congratulated by Darlene Hard after their 1957 Wimbledon singles final.

the last woman to realize that gigantic feat in 1952—53. Prior to her, the last female to do it was Wills Moody, who went one better from 1927–29.

Afterwards, Gibson stunned the audience at the West Side Tennis Club by announcing she would be taking the following year off to pursue a career as a singer, something she had been dabbling with for the previous year. She had even recorded an album of standard songs in 1958. Her singing aspirations did not pan out, but Gibson was able to make some significant money when she played a pro tour against the Floridian Karol Fageros in 1959–60.

Fageros was a capable competitor who had achieved a No. 5 American ranking in 1957. But Gibson crushed her old friend 114-4 in their one-sided series of matches. On that tour, it was announced that Fageros would make $30,000 while the major drawcard Gibson made $100,000.

Her business group called "Althea Gibson Enterprises" launched a follow-up pro tour for the two Americans that failed miserably financially as they performed for scant audiences. That was essentially

Gibson's legacy is far reaching, but more than anything else it is about the powerful role she played in tennis history by breaking down the color barriers.

the end of Gibson's tennis career at 33. No more offers were on the horizon so she courageously turned to golf and tried to make an impact on the greens. Between 1963 and 1971 she played 148 tournaments but earned a mere $19,727 despite her extraordinary dedication.

She played more golf tournaments deep into the 1970s with little success, competed in the U.S. Open tennis mixed doubles once with Arthur Ashe, appeared in small tennis tournaments and exhibitions periodically. Off-court she was married a couple of times, with both ending in divorce. In her waning years, Gibson became largely reclusive in her modest New Jersey surroundings.

Toward the end of her life, Gibson was broke. Friends stepped in to help and writer Paul Fein wrote a piece in *Tennis Week* magazine asking the tennis community to lend a helping hand financially to enable Gibson to pay her bills and bolster her spirits. Her health deteriorated and her weight dropped dangerously from about 150 pounds down to 100. But the money from fans and old friends poured in, and a legendary figure concluded her life with dignity. At 78, she passed away in 2003. Sixteen years later, a statue of Gibson was erected outside Arthur Ashe Stadium to permanently honor her at the U.S. Open.

Gibson's legacy is far reaching, but more than anything else it is about the powerful role she played in tennis history by breaking down the color barriers and opening doors for future generations of Black competitors.

Althea Gibson achieved her success and prominence entirely on her own terms. What she wrote in her memoir, *I Always Wanted to Be Somebody*, tells us everything we need to know about how she looked at herself and the world. Her message was, "I've never regarded myself as a crusader. I am always glad when something I do turns out to be helpful … I don't consciously beat the drums for any special cause, not even the cause of the Negro in the United States … our best chance to advance is to prove ourselves as individuals."

Gibson practiced what she preached and established herself unequivocally as an all-time great American player, all the while dealing with the burdens of breaking the color barrier.

King on her way to beating British left-hander Ann Jones to reach her first Wimbledon singles final in 1963.

BILLIE JEAN KING

Full name	Billie Jean Moffitt King
Birthdate	22 November 1943
Place of birth	Long Beach, California
Major singles titles	6 Wimbledon (1966–68, 1972–73, 1975); 4 U.S. Championships/U.S. Open (1967, 1971–72, 1974); Australian Championships (1968); French Open (1972)

A standout even among the immortals of American tennis, Billie Jean King has comprehensively influenced the sport on countless levels. Few have even tried to venture where she has gone outside the arena.

Others played significant roles in popularizing tennis, and some loomed larger than the game. But King is unsurpassed as a multi-faceted leader, indispensable mover and shaker, and the most transcendent American female athlete of all time.

She came out of California and conquered the world, demonstrating unequivocally that she was a complete player, placing a premium not only on singles but doubles as well. In fact, her unbridled enthusiasm was accompanied by a relentless dedication to her craft. King's largest dreams were fulfilled because she was willing to rise above and beyond to meet the toughest of challenges.

An endlessly probing match player, King was the quintessential serve-and-volley practitioner of her era alongside Australia's Margaret Court, moving forward unhesitatingly to display a dazzling array of skills at the net. On the volley she was nearly flawless. Her backhand volley ranks among the very best of all time, although her forehand groundstroke could be vulnerable.

In a 2024 interview for this book, King told me, "My generation with the wooden rackets were taught incorrectly, totally contrary to the

In 1966, King shares a playful moment in Southern California with renowned player and coach Pancho Segura.

way they teach today. The science now is so much better."

Many remember King for her wide range of pursuits off the court that brought such benefits to the sport, but her prolific accomplishments as a player are too easily forgotten.

Altogether, she collected 39 major titles between 1961 and 1980. She took

12 of those crowns in singles, including six championship runs at Wimbledon, four at the U.S Championships/Open, and one each at the Australian Championships and French Open. Perhaps she was an even better doubles player, capturing 16 majors in women's doubles and another 11 in mixed doubles. On three different occasions – in 1967 and 1973 at Wimbledon and also at the 1967 U.S. Championships – she won the "Triple Crown" by sweeping the singles, doubles, and mixed doubles championships. As of 2025, she stood in third place on the all-time women's list, behind Margaret Court and Martina Navratilova for total Grand Slam titles.

Raised in a middle-class Southern California family, Billie Jean Moffitt, the daughter of a firefighter father and a nurturing mother, realized from a very young age that her goals in life were extraordinary. As she wrote in her 2023 autobiography, *All In,* "I can't remember a time when I didn't have a restlessness, an ambition, an urgency."

She started playing tennis as a fifth-grade student when she was ten. As an eighth grader King discovered she was nearsighted and wearing glasses would be a necessity. But, as she told me in 2024, "God gave me and my brother [a former professional baseball player] really good eyesight. I wear glasses but I have 20/10 vision. To this day I can see the ball really well."

It wasn't simply wearing spectacles that allowed King to envision a future for herself in tennis; it was an insatiable desire to be a central figure in tennis that gave King clarity of vision. At 15 bordering on 16, she started taking lessons from the legendary Alice Marble. Their brief dynamic player-coach relationship left an indelible mark on King.

By her senior year in high school in 1960, she was the No. 4 ranked player in the United States at the age of 17. King made a memorable trip to Great Britain to make her debut at Wimbledon in 1961, and, lo and behold, came away with the first of her Grand Slam titles in doubles alongside Karen Hantze Susman.

That was a seminal moment in her life. More than simply claiming her first major title, she had established a relationship with Wimbledon that would stretch across the decades. Eighteen years later, she joined forces with Martina Navratilova to capture the women's doubles championships for the tenth time on the hallowed lawns in Great Britain. More significantly, it was her record 20th crown overall at Wimbledon in a spectacular 19-year span at the shrine.

King's reverence for Wimbledon was boundless. A pivotal victory for her at the shrine came in 1962 when she upended defending champion Margaret Court in the second round. King became the first unseeded player ever to topple a No. 1 seed in the 86-year history of the tournament.

In both 1963 and 1964, she was the second ranked player in the United States. The following year, she was co-ranked No. 1 with the Texan Nancy Richey. But it was in 1966, the year she turned 23, that King came of age. Seeded fourth at Wimbledon, King upended the top-seeded Smith [Court] in the semifinals 6-3, 6-3, and backed up that big win by overcoming Maria Bueno, the elegant Brazilian who was seeded second. King defeated Bueno 6-3, 3-6, 6-1 in the final with a signature performance for her first singles title at a major.

By the end of that year, King had cemented her status as the leading women's player in the United States and the best in the world. She won ten singles titles that season and 57 of 65 matches. In 1967, King took her game to an even loftier level, defending her singles crown at Wimbledon and securing her first U.S. Championships singles title.

King in those days was unassailable. Fittingly, she returned to Great Britain to win Wimbledon for a third year in a row at the first Open edition on those hallowed grounds in 1968. She celebrated a third successive year as the No. 1 ranked woman in tennis.

At 25, she was at the very top of the tennis mountain. But her 1969 and 1970 seasons were less stellar. King needed one of her many knee surgeries later in that 1970 season and missed the U.S. Open. But she played an indispensable role in the formation of a women's tour and the creation of the "Original Nine". Nine leading players, led by King as the superstar, signed $1 professional contracts with the charismatic and ingenious promoter Gladys M. Heldman to play a female-only tournament in Houston at the end of September. They were combating the male-dominated tennis establishment intent on offering them insulting tournament prize money that was eight to one – or sometimes more – in favor of the men.

That tournament was sponsored by Virginia Slims, a subsidiary of Philip Morris, Co. Joe Cullman was the CEO of Philip Morris and Heldman persuaded him to get his company to put up the $7,500 in prize money for the initial tournament. As Julie Heldman, one of the nine players who signed on and the daughter of Gladys Heldman, wrote in her book *Driven,* "We succeeded because we had an unbeatable combination of leaders, our Holy Trinity [Gladys Heldman, Billie Jean King, and Joe Cullman]

who were all deeply committed to the success of the women's pro tour."

A full-fledged circuit emerged the next year for women. As King wrote in *All In,* "Tennis players are entertainers, and, as such, we should be paid the same regardless of how many sets we play or what our gender is. We never claimed that we were better than the men … women were putting on just as good a show. Now we were proving it."

King expanded on her thoughts on the importance of the Original Nine in her interview with me 50 years later for usopen.org. She said, "We, as the Original Nine, were not doing it for ourselves. It was a real team effort. Without it, I would not be who I am. Never in 100 years would I have had the life I have without the nine of us sticking together."

King fully understood that promoting the new tour was a serious responsibility, but also knew she had to play prodigiously as well. Across that landmark season of 1971, she became the first female athlete ever to make $100,000 in prize money for a year, amassing $117,000, securing 17 titles and winning 112 singles matches.

Speaking about her monetary achievement, King told me in a 2020 usta.com interview, "If you look at what I was making, it was more than a lot of the great baseball players. I made $117,000. So I was in the higher echelon, even

Her career was overflowing with challenges, on and off the court.

for men's sports. That is what people understand. They understood money."

Meanwhile, King understood how difficult it could be to play her best brand of tennis while simultaneously doing everything in her power to create a thriving workplace for women on the tour. As she told me in 2024 when reflecting on the years leading up to a separate women's tour, "My generation was the transition generation, taking the sport from amateur to pro. If I wanted to lead, I was not going to win as much. I had to ask myself some very hard questions because I knew I would have won more if I had not been so concerned about the changing of the sport. What did I want to say about myself – that I was a champion and won all of these Grand Slam tournaments, or that I tried to change the sport for the better and make it more inclusive? It was a very conscious decision I made that I would rather take the game to a different place than win more championships."

Her career was overflowing with challenges, on and off the court. But King in 1972 – coming off her magnificent 1971 campaign – played the

A year before securing her first singles title at Wimbledon, King lost in the 1965 semifinals to Maria Bueno.

finest tennis of her career at 28, taking three of the four majors including her lone French Open singles title, capturing ten titles, winning 87 of 99 matches.

As she told me in 2024 for this book, "From age 26 or 27 to about 31 is when

In a dazzling performance on Centre Court, King granted Goolagong only one game in two sets to win her sixth Wimbledon singles title in 1975.

you hit your high point because you have so much experience. I had played a lot of tennis in 1971, so in '72 I was hitting my stride. I could have won all four majors that year but I didn't play the Australian Open. I played the Virginia Slims of San Francisco at the same time. Helping the circuit and professional tennis was more important to me than trying to win the Australian that year, but my chances of winning all four [for a Grand Slam] would have been extremely high because I was playing so well in 1972."

The highlight for King was her French Open triumph. She took apart Evonne Goolagong 6-3, 6-3 in the final and did not lose a set over the fortnight, but in King's mind it was her practice sessions leading up to Roland-Garros with Chris Evert in Florida that enabled her to prevail in Paris. As she told me in 2024, "We hit for a week. It doesn't get any better than that. Chris Evert is the reason I won the 1972 French Open. She couldn't go since she was still in high school, but she helped me a lot to get ready."

But perhaps her largest contribution to the sport that year was persuading U.S. Open Tournament Director Billy Talbert that the women needed to be paid equally in 1973 and telling him she could help line up a sponsor to make it happen. Ban Deodorant put up the $55,000 required to bring about the prize money parity, and, thanks largely to King, Court made $25,000 for winning the 1973 U.S. Open – the same amount as John Newcombe got for taking the men's title.

In 1973, King garnered her fifth singles title at Wimbledon over Evert and added the women's and mixed doubles titles for her last "triple". It was on the eve of the tournament that King spearheaded the formation of the Women's Tennis Association (WTA) and became the first president of the player organization. Three months later, she confronted Bobby Riggs in the famed "Battle of the Sexes". Riggs had routed Margaret Court 6-2, 6-1 in the "Mother's Day Massacre" that spring in California.

That was a blow to the steadily advancing women's game, and King knew she would have to remedy the situation swiftly, agreeing to meet Riggs on 20 September 1973 at the Houston Astrodome in front of 30,472 fans, and millions more watching worldwide on television. King, 29, could not afford to lose to a 55-year-old hustler who had played his best tennis decades earlier in the late 1930s (he won a "Triple" at Wimbledon in 1939) and early forties. She took apart Riggs 6-4, 6-3, 6-3 in what may well have been the most important match she ever played.

King was flourishing with more on her plate than ever before. In that same crowded 1973 calendar, she founded World Team Tennis with her husband Larry (whom she married in 1965) and the league was born in May of 1974. WTT, featuring big-name players of both sexes, was the brainchild of King. Sixteen franchises competed from cities as diverse as New York and Los Angeles, Boston and Baltimore, Cleveland and Chicago. King was the player/coach of the Philadelphia Freedoms. In the coming years she played for the New York Sets/Apples. Among those who appeared in WTT were Evert, Navratilova, Connors, McEnroe, and the Williams sisters. King's full commitment was critical. The league lasted until 2021.

Meanwhile, King in 1974 was conflicted about whether she had the energy and enthusiasm after the grueling WTT season to play the U.S. Open, but ultimately chose to participate. She faced Goolagong in the final on the lawns in New York, succeeding 3-6, 6-3, 7-5 in front of a capacity crowd enraptured by the creativity of both players. King rallied spectacularly from 0-3 in the final set to win a spellbinding showdown.

Reflecting on that encounter in 2005, King told me in an interview for *Tennis Week* magazine, "That was the first year we had a standing room only crowd in the stadium at Forest Hills and the first time I saw the U.S. Open with so

King at 72 remained boundlessly energetic, ambitious, and happy as she pursued a wide range of goals.

much electricity in the air, with people sitting down on the grass at court-side in front of the area where the box seat holders sat. The stadium was absolute chock-a-block full. For tennis, that was a huge step forward with so many people watching and appreciating us."

King took on Goolagong again in the Wimbledon final ten months later, ruthlessly recording a 6-0, 6-1 triumph in 38 immaculate minutes. Totally on song, King took her sixth and last singles title at the All England Club and her 12th and final Grand Slam singles title.

The 31-year-old, 5'5" dynamo announced her retirement from singles, but reconsidered and returned late in the 1976 season. There were some successes in the years ahead including semifinal runs at Wimbledon in 1982–83. She was 39 in the latter appearance. But unlike Jimmy Connors – who cherished his semifinal run at the 1991 U.S. Open when he was 39 – King was dissatisfied about not winning it all.

She lost in three sets to Evert in the first of those Centre Court semifinals and was beaten by teenager Andrea Jaeger the following year. She told me in 2024, "When I lost those matches, it made me irritated. In '82 against Chris I could have beaten her if I had

Tennis has seldom witnessed such a trailblazer. The U.S. Open facility was renamed the USTA Billie Jean King National Tennis Center.

believed in myself more. When you get older there is that little doubt in the back of your mind that you are not good enough. You have got to finish and win the tournament. Don't give me that semis or finals stuff. Finish."

A few years later, she filed for divorce from Larry King in 1987. She had been outed in 1981 by her former lover and hairdresser Marilyn Barnett, who filed a palimony suit. King fought it and eventually was victorious in court. She eventually settled into a long-term relationship with former South African player Ilana Kloss, who won the 1976 U.S. Open in women's doubles. They married in 2018.

Tennis has seldom witnessed such a trailblazer. In 2006, the U.S. Open facility was renamed the USTA Billie Jean King National Tennis Center. Serenaded in Arthur Ashe Stadium on a festive evening by Connors, McEnroe, Evert, and Venus Williams, the 62-year-old King clenched her fists joyously, shook her head incredulously, and celebrated the honor unabashedly.

There was more. In 2020, the Fed Cup international women's team competition was renamed Billie Jean King Cup. She had led the United States to victory in the inaugural year of the competition back in 1963, and contributed to subsequent American triumphs in 1967, 1977, 1978, and 1979, even serving as player-captain a few times. In 1995 she became non-playing captain and guided the U.S. to triumphs in 1996, 1997, and 2000.

In the years to come, King was the recipient of some extraordinary honors. In 2009, she was awarded a Presidential Medal of Freedom by President Barack Obama, and 15 years later became the first individual female athlete to be awarded the Congressional Gold Medal when Joe Biden was President. She became the first woman ever to be awarded a star for sports entertainment on the Hollywood Walk of Fame in 2025.

When I asked how she would define her legacy in 2024, the 81-year-old King responded, "Legacy is what other people think, not what I think. But what I am going to ask myself at the end is: what contributions did I leave here to make this world a better place? I am not finished yet, but that is the essence of what we should ask ourselves."

Unquestionably, Billie Jean King, regardless of her wide range of pursuits, is, and always will be, synonymous with tennis.

In 1964, Ashe was playing college tennis for UCLA, winning the prestigious NCAA Championships the following year.

Arthur Ashe

Full name	Arthur Robert Ashe Jr.
Birthdate	10 July 1943; died 6 February 1993
Place of birth	Richmond, Virginia
Major singles titles	U.S. Open (1968); Australian Open (1970); Wimbledon (1975)

A man who was considerably larger than the game he played for a living, a champion who comported himself with remarkable self-restraint and composure, a uniquely charismatic player with imagination and flair, Arthur Ashe was a beloved figure and an iconic athlete to boot. He was admired by even casual observers of sport, appreciative of his many extraordinary qualities as both a player and a human being.

As the first Black man ever to secure a Grand Slam singles championship – he was victorious at three of the four majors between 1968 and 1975 – and a stalwart performer on three consecutive championship U.S. Davis Cup teams from 1968–70, Ashe took great pride in becoming one of the sport's central figures.

Ashe was a universally appealing player celebrated for his audacious big hitting and a capacity to bring audiences onto their feet with his dazzling displays. The explosiveness of his tennis combined with his implacable on-court demeanor set him apart.

The deep reverence among fans for Ashe was never more apparent than when he triumphed at Wimbledon in 1975 less than a week before he turned 32, when he knew there would be precious few opportunities left to lift the world's most coveted trophy and thus underline his status as a player of lasting importance.

Sprawled out on court at Wimbledon in 1965, Ashe peaked at the shrine in 1975.

As he told me in a 1985 interview, "That was the capstone of my career."

The 1975 campaign for the 6'1", 155-pound Ashe had gone remarkably well leading up to Wimbledon. He had already recorded five tournament triumphs in the first half of the season, most significantly taking the WCT Finals in Dallas where he defeated Bjorn Borg in the title-round contest across four sets.

Heading into Wimbledon quietly confident as the No. 6 seed, he conceded only two sets in his first four matches before coming from behind to topple the No. 3 seed Borg 2-6, 6-4, 8-6, 6-1 for a place in the penultimate round. That was no mean feat for Ashe to beat the Swede, who would win the tournament the next five years.

Ashe then collided with No. 16 seed Tony Roche, overcoming the tenacious left-handed Australian in five sets.

Now the dynamic American found himself pitted against countryman Jimmy Connors in a highly charged final-round appointment – the first between two Americans since Kramer defeated Tom Brown in 1947. Connors was the defending champion. The swashbuckling left-hander had looked invincible in reaching the final without losing a set, and had seemed untouchable in cutting down the big-serving southpaw Roscoe Tanner 6-4, 6-1, 6-4 in a breathtaking semifinal.

Adding to the drama of the occasion was the fact that Connors was suing Ashe – the President of the ATP – for libel and slander. His manager, Bill Riordan, filed the suit two days before

Wimbledon began, but not long after withdrew it. Ashe played the most cerebral match of his career. The night before he confronted Connors on the fabled Centre Court, he had dined with a number of players and friends including his manager and close friend Donald Dell, Charlie Pasarell, and Fred McNair. He also consulted two other players and former doubles partners he had known for a long time – Dennis Ralston and Marty Riessen.

There was a consensus that Ashe should produce a different brand of tennis than was his custom. He would have played into the hands of Connors if he elected to come at his rival with all guns blazing. Tanner tried in vain to blow Connors off the court with an onslaught of power.

Rather than blasting his groundstrokes as hard as he would have liked, Ashe released a magnificent mixture of chips, dinks, cagey slices, and shots designed to disrupt the rhythm of Connors. He lobbed with under-spin off the backhand more skillfully than he had ever done before. Moreover, he served with supreme intelligence, resisting the impulse to release his biggest deliveries and making excellent use of his slice serve in the deuce court which went wide to the Connors two-handed backhand and opened up the court.

Ashe had lost all three of his previous encounters with Connors in the finals of the U.S. Pro Championships in 1973 along with the 1973 and 1974 South African Opens. But he confounded a compatriot more than nine years younger.

Ashe took the first two sets with sweeping self-assurance at the cost of two games, dropped a hard-fought third set, and then trailed 0-3 in the fourth set. But he stuck to his tactics and swept six of the last seven games to complete a 6-1, 6-1, 5-7, 6-4 victory in style. It was indeed the crowning moment of his career. At long last, on July 5, 1975 in his ninth appearance at the shrine, he had secured the single most important tournament in tennis.

As Ashe told me in a 1989 interview for *World Tennis* magazine, he felt, in the only Wimbledon final he ever contested, that he was in the zone, that place when great players believe they are unbeatable on given days. He explained, "When you're in the zone, your perspective of time is completely warped. I'll tell you what snapped me out of that time warp against Connors. After the second set I looked up at the clock for the first time in the match and it was 2:41PM. We started shortly after 2PM and seeing how little time had elapsed snapped me out of whatever I was in. In hindsight I wish I had never looked at the clock, because that put me back on the left side of my brain, the logical part. Playing in the zone is playing on the right side of your brain; it is creative, mystical, letting your body do what it knows how to do. Logic, rationality and reason don't interfere. I really think if I had not looked up at that clock I would have beaten Connors in straight sets."

Tennis fans rejoiced after Ashe meticulously pulled off one of the monumental sports upsets. Ashe told me in 1985 for a column I was writing for *World Tennis* magazine that people would constantly approach him to express the joy they found in his victory over Connors.

He said, "I might be standing in an elevator or walking down the street, and somebody comes up to me and says something about it. Among whites they say it was one of the most memorable moments in sports. Among Blacks, I've had quite a few say it was up there with [boxer] Joe Louis in his prime and [baseball player] Jackie Robinson breaking in with the Dodgers in 1947."

That Wimbledon championship run, culminating with the stunning upset of Connors, is preeminent in the minds of Ashe observers. But he did not make history of such magnitude accidentally. It was the result of a lifelong dedication to his craft.

Born in Richmond, Virginia, Ashe was raised predominantly by his father, after his mother died when he was six years old. During the early stages of his childhood, Ashe got the measles, whooping cough, chicken pox, diptheria, and any number of other ailments.

He started playing tennis at the age of seven. As he progressed and played junior tournaments in his home state, Ashe came to the attention of Dr. Robert Walter Johnson, the man who had played such a critical role in the shaping of Althea Gibson's tennis evolution. "Dr. J." had his home court and training facility in Lynchburg, Virginia.

He went to the University of California, Los Angeles (UCLA) and won the coveted NCAA Championships in 1965, but played men's tournaments throughout his tenure there, achieving a No. 6 ranking in the nation in 1963 and moving up three spots a year later.

In that crucial transition year of 1965 when he rounded out his college career, Ashe celebrated a seminal moment at

Striking a backhand at a WCT tournament in Rotterdam during his signature season of 1975, Ashe was superb off that side.

Ashe is joined by the Dutchman Tom Okker (far left) prior to a doubles exhibition in 1975, nearly seven years after they met in the U.S. Open singles final.

the U.S. Championships. Facing the defending champion Roy Emerson at Forest Hills in the quarterfinals, he gave the exhilarated crowd palpable joy by serving thunderbolts, making outright backhand return winners, and putting away volleys elegantly. Ashe upended the Australian in four spectacular sets to reach his first major semifinal. He concluded the year at No. 2 in the U.S.

In 1966, he remained the No. 2 ranked player in the United States and made it to his first final at a Grand Slam singles championship, losing to Emerson at the Australian Championships. A year later, he finished a third season in a row as the No. 2 American, and reached a second straight final at the Australian Championships.

When "Open Tennis" commenced in 1968, he began peaking auspiciously. For the first time, the leading professionals like Rod Laver, Ken Rosewall, and one of Ashe's mentors, Pancho Gonzalez, were allowed to return to the glamorous Grand Slam settings and compete against the best of the amateurs like Ashe and his U.S. Davis Cup teammate Clark Graebner. Ashe joined Graebner in the Wimbledon semifinals, losing to the eventual champion Laver.

Thereafter, across a stupendous summer, Ashe was almost unbeatable, winning a couple of tournaments on grass courts including the U.S. Championships in Brookline, Massachusetts in a five-set thriller over Davis Cup teammate Bob Lutz.

Buoyed by those successes, he came to Forest Hills for the inaugural U.S. Open seeded fifth. The top-seeded Laver was in his quarterfinal bracket. Ashe had not yet beaten Laver and would not do so until 1974. But Laver suffered a shocking fourth-round defeat against No. 16 seed Cliff Drysdale, turning the tournament upside down.

Ashe was serving in the United States Army, so the umpires would always announce "Game, Lieutenant Ashe". He virtually owned Drysdale and proceeded to bury the South African under an avalanche of searing aces and blockbuster backhand winners. He advanced in four sets to the semifinals against Graebner, coming from behind to beat his familiar rival 4-6, 8-6, 7-5, 6-2.

In the final, Ashe found himself up against the "Flying Dutchman" Tom Okker, a fleet-footed topspin artist. Behind 26 aces and countless blazing winners, Ashe captured the U.S. Open title with a 14-12, 5-7, 6-3, 3–6, 6-3 triumph. Not long after that victory, *Life* magazine ran a photo of Ashe on the cover and a poignant photo inside with his arm around his proud and teary-eyed father. At 25, he was the first United States Open champion. As an amateur, he could not accept the champion's prize money of $14,500, but his achievement was life-altering and made him feel like a million bucks.

Perhaps Herbert Warren Wind in the *New Yorker* best put the Ashe U.S. Open success story into perspective, writing, "I can't conceive of a more popular victory. Ashe is not only a very fine young man but a very rare young man. Intelligent, calm, honest and natural, he is the antithesis of the spoiled American tennis hero."

He was also an electrifying player with one of the biggest and best serves of his era bolstered by a magnificent backhand volley and an explosive backhand groundstroke which the fans always enjoyed watching him artistically unleash.

As journalist John McPhee wrote in his 1969 book *Levels of the Game,* "Tennis players fear Ashe's backhand … Ashe loves the movement of the backhand, because the follow-through does not cramp the arm into the body but just the opposite – opens both arms wide and high, so that the stroke ends in the stance of the Winged Victory."

As the curtain closed on a tumultuous 1968, Ashe had another signature accomplishment, leading the U.S. Davis Cup team to their first triumph in five years as the Americans defeated Australia in the final. He would propel them to victory again in 1969 and 1970. Ashe at last climbed to No. 1 in the U.S. in 1968.

It was an arduous task for Ashe to live up to the previous year's accomplishments. In 1969 he was a semifinalist at Wimbledon and the U.S. Open but slipped to second in the U.S., behind the swiftly improving Stan Smith. In 1970, Ashe finished as the third-best American behind Cliff Richey and Smith, despite winning his second major at the Australian Open.

He was a strikingly potent performer in the first half of the 1970s.

He was a strikingly potent performer over the first half of the 1970s. In 1972, he nearly took a second U.S. Open title, ousting Stan Smith and Richey to reach the final at Forest Hills, establishing a two sets to one lead in the final against Romania's Ilie Nastase. Ashe was ahead 4-2 in the fourth set before the gifted Nastase rallied to win in five sets. Despondently, Ashe sat in his chair afterwards, waiting for the presentation ceremony to commence, holding his head in his hands as his eyes welled up.

Four months later, I interviewed Ashe at the Albert Hall in London while he was there for a tournament, asking if he had any lingering thoughts on that agonizing setback. He replied, "Sometimes I wake up in the middle of the night thinking about it. I guess I wanted it too badly."

Ashe had a few more very good years in 1973 and 1974, maintaining his status as one of the leading Americans and as a regular occupant of the world's top ten. Meanwhile, he made his first trip to the South African Open in 1973, spending 12 days in that country, reaching the singles final and winning the doubles, trying in

On his way to producing one of the great upsets in tennis history against Jimmy Connors in the Wimbledon final of 1975.

his thoughtful way to fight apartheid. As Richard Evans wrote in *World Tennis* magazine, "Neither before nor during his trip would Ashe indulge in any inflammatory criticism of South Africa or its policies … He had no illusions … He knew that he was wielding a double-edged sword that could cut as deeply into the wall of apartheid as it could dull the ferocity of world opinion."

That journey to South Africa was a triumph stretching well beyond the lines of a tennis court. Be that as it may, his record in 1975 was outstanding as he won 103 matches and eight tournaments, including the coveted Wimbledon crown. Most authorities honored Ashe with the No. 1 world ranking and the USTA placed him above Connors as the top-ranked American.

Ashe's triumph over Connors in that 1975 final was immensely popular.

Ashe told writer Barry Lorge how it felt to be regarded by the experts as the best player in the world after so many years living in that vicinity. He said, "It's the pinnacle. You're on top of the mountain. Forty years from now I can tell my grandchildren that in 1975 I was the best tennis player in the whole world."

After slipping to third in the U.S. in 1976, Ashe was idle in 1977 while

Ashe belongs among an elite class of American athletes. He was an intellectual who read prodigiously and spoke with an eloquence that added substantial weight to his words.

recovering from heel surgery and 1978 was another quiet year. But he was resurgent in 1979 at 35. In January, he had two match points in the final of the Grand Prix Masters indoors at Madison Square Garden in New York. He then made it to the finals of both Philadelphia and Memphis. In early August he, shockingly, suffered a heart attack weeks after turning 36 when he was ranked No. 7 in the world. Always slender, fit, and healthy, Ashe could never have envisioned such a fate. He did not compete again, announcing his retirement in 1980.

Ashe served as the captain of the U.S. Davis Cup team from 1981–85, and his teams – spearheaded by John McEnroe – were twice victorious in that span. In 1988, Ashe was diagnosed as H.I.V. positive resulting from a blood transfusion during a second heart procedure in 1983. He passed away on 6 February 1993 at the age of 49 and was memorialized not only in Richmond, Virginia where he grew up, but in New York where he had resided for much of his adult life. Four years after he passed away, the new U.S. Open stadium was fittingly named after him.

Ashe belongs among an elite class of American athletes. He was an intellectual who read prodigiously and spoke with an eloquence that added substantial weight to his words. Ashe appreciated the fact that Althea Gibson opened up more than a few doors for him as the first Black player to claim the premier prizes, but Ashe was performing in an era when the game was much higher profile. In many ways, his task was tougher than Gibson's, but he handled it commendably.

Arthur Ashe was ardently admired by the players and public alike, and widely respected as a man who understood who he was and how he wanted to conduct himself in life. There have been champions from the United States with wider resumes and greater arsenals, individuals who were more consistent in their craftsmanship. But as a human being and leader who spoke softly yet seemed to be heard loudly, he belonged in a class of his own.

19-year-old Smith at Wimbledon in 1966 when he was still getting his feet wet.

STAN SMITH

Full name	Stanley Roger Smith
Birthdate	14 December 1946
Place of birth	Pasadena, California
Major singles titles	U.S. Open (1971); Wimbledon (1972)

For all who were present for it back in 1973, the
final-round contest between Stan Smith and
Arthur Ashe in the WCT Finals at Moody Coliseum
in Dallas, Texas left a lasting impression.

Smith was leading two sets to one in this best of five-set clash, with Ashe serving at 4-5 and deuce in the fourth. Smith chased a shot that landed short in the court, which Ashe erroneously thought his opponent had not reached until the ball bounced twice. Ashe lost that point and, after saving a match point, bowed out 6-3, 6-3, 4-6, 6-4 against his respected rival, but questions lingered about the controversial point.

Afterwards at the presentation ceremony, a classy Ashe said, "I want to say now, before the rumors start about whether the ball was hit on the first or second bounce, that if Stan says he got it, he got it."

Smith said a short time later, "When I shook hands with Arthur at the net, I didn't feel like I had just won the WCT title. I was just hoping the ball had really been 'up' as I wouldn't want to win on a wrong decision, especially against Arthur who is such a good friend. That was why I was relieved when the TV replay proved I got it on the first bounce."

That incident in Dallas was symbolic of Smith's entire tennis career. He was a genuine sportsman and an uncomplicated man with no pretenses and no discernible shades of gray. Smith valued integrity and fundamental decency more than anything else, had a thoroughly clean slate as a competitor, and

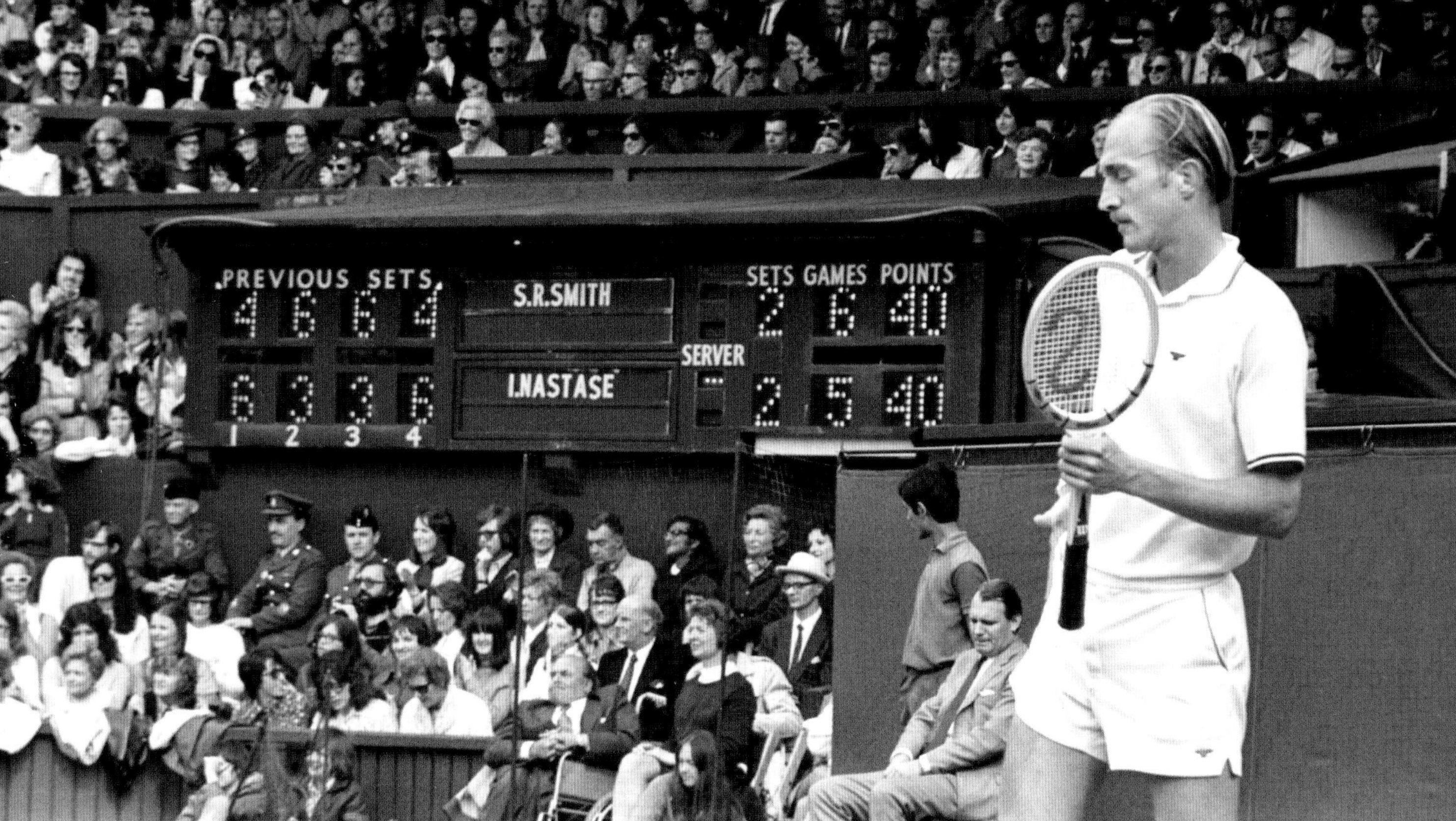

Smith is two points away from upending Ilie Nastase in a classic 1972 Wimbledon final.

a conscience that guided him incessantly through both the good and bad stretches of a great career.

Brought up on the hard courts of California, Smith started later than many of his peers, but dedicated himself fully to an attacking game and concluded his junior career by capturing the National 18s Championships in 1964, which he used as a stepping stone toward success in the men's game. Smith established himself as the No. 14 American men's player in 1965, rising to No. 11 the following season. By 1967, playing college tennis for the University of Southern California (USC), he surged to No. 7 in the nation, winning six singles titles that season.

Smith was exceptionally tall for his time at 6'4", but his capacity to make low volleys from his shoelaces was extraordinary. Moreover, his serve, released with a smooth and repeatable motion, was utterly reliable. The vast majority of top players in that era stood around 6 feet tall or even shorter. In his junior year at USC, he claimed the most coveted prize in college tennis with a triumph at the 1968 NCAA Championships. That was a banner year as Smith was victorious at eight tournaments, moving up to No. 3 in the U.S. Moreover, he made his debut on the triumphant United States Davis Cup team by contributing a doubles victory alongside Bob Lutz in the Challenge Round win over Australia.

But if there was a turning-point year that gave Smith a much loftier status, it was surely 1969. From that season through 1973, Smith celebrated a five-year period of peak productivity, starting with an important triumph at the 1969 U.S. Championships in Brookline, Massachusetts.

Competing on grass courts at the fabled Longwood Cricket Club, Smith managed to fend off Australian left-hander Ray Ruffels 12-10 in the fifth set of his quarterfinal, and then made a gallant comeback to defeat countryman Charlie Pasarell 4-6, 2-6, 6-2, 8-6,15-13. Toughened by those skirmishes, he defeated doubles partner Bob Lutz 9-7, 6-3, 6-1 for what was then his biggest tournament triumph.

When I asked him to put that achievement in perspective 40 years later, Smith said, "That was when I thought maybe I did belong with the top players. It was a great confidence booster and it helped me in the following years."

Smith finished a stellar 1969 campaign as the top-ranked player in the U.S., winning 75 of 90 matches and eight titles, underlining his supremacy with winning head-to-head records over all of his key American rivals including Ashe, Pasarell, Graebner, and Cliff Richey. That set the stage for another outstanding season in 1970, despite the fact that Richey narrowly eclipsed him for the top spot in the country.

He dropped to second on the 1970 American list, but ended that year on the highest possible note by winning the first edition ever of The Masters year-end, round robin event in Tokyo, featuring an elite six-player field including the venerable Australians Rod Laver and Ken Rosewall along with Ashe. Smith upended both Australian legends and, with a 4-1 record, walked away with a significant title. Laver had secured his second Grand Slam the previous year and Rosewall had taken the U.S. Open title a few months earlier.

As Smith recalls, "I had been postponing the military draft for almost a year. My birthday is December 14 and that was the day I played Rosewall. We knew that the winner of our match was going to win The Masters and I managed to beat Ken to ensure that I won the tournament. Jack Kramer led 10,000 Japanese in singing Happy Birthday for me. I flew to L.A. on the 15th. They gave me 'excess leave' which allowed me to go home for Christmas. I started serving after that."

Smith would remain in the army until the autumn of 1972 but was permitted to play a lot of high-quality tennis during those years. He returned to the top of American tennis in 1971 when he reached the quarterfinals of the French Open, the final of Wimbledon and then collected the U.S. Open title.

At that U.S. Open, which he won on the Forest Hills grass at the West Side Tennis Club in New York, the No. 2 seed Smith's unshakable disposition and the soundness of his percentage serve-and-volley playbook was fully on display. He stopped 1968 finalist Tom Okker in a hard-fought five-set semifinal encounter and then came from behind to beat the Czech Jan Kodes in a four-set final. Okker was formidable on every surface and Kodes had accounted for both Newcombe (the top seed) and the No. 3 seed Ashe. Smith stopped Kodes 3-6, 6-3, 6-2, 7-6 – prevailing 5-3 in the old "Sudden Death" tiebreaker.

Smith felt that his impeccable tiebreak record at that tournament carried him to a breakthrough Grand Slam title. He recalled, "That was only the second year of the tiebreaker. I was in five tiebreakers during that tournament and I won them all. That was sort of an indicator that I was pretty confident."

Another factor working in Smith's favor was a chance meeting with his old coach Pancho Segura, a great professional player in the 1950s and '60s, and one of the game's strategic masterminds. Segura, who coached Jimmy Connors for many years, gave Smith some astute advice just prior to his assignment against Kodes when they serendipitously crossed paths. Segura advised Smith to put pressure on Kodes's second serve by running around his backhand to unleash forehand returns, use the lob when Kodes closed in tight on the net, and release kick serves to the Kodes forehand to exploit his opponent's continental forehand grip.

As Smith told me in 2024, "Segura didn't have the physical attributes of the players in his era so he had to think his way through matches. He helped me to think my way through matches like the one with Kodes. He was a genius on the mental side of the game."

Smith was not only the best American competitor in 1971 but, according to most experts, No. 2 in the world behind John Newcombe.

In 1972, however, he was the pacesetter of the sport, winning seven tournaments, performing magnificently from the beginning of the year until the end. But his finest and most character-defining work was done in realizing a lifelong dream by ruling at Wimbledon, and leading the United States to an astonishing Davis Cup victory.

At Wimbledon, the top-seeded Smith dropped only three sets in six matches on his way to a final-round appointment against Romanian Ilie Nastase. They were polar opposites in terms of temperament and playing style, with Smith stoically trying to impose himself with his reliable serve-and-volley game, while the mercurial Nastase countered with his dazzling shotmaking artistry.

In a pendulum swinging skirmish, Smith found himself in a harrowing fifth set. Serving at 4-4 but down 0-30, his forehand volley off the frame fell over the net for a very fortunate winner. He held on in that critical ninth game and then Nastase saved two match points on his way to 5-5. Ultimately, Smith found an opening with Nastase serving in the 12th game. Nastase took a 40-0 lead, lost four points in a row, saved a third match point but then missed an easy backhand overhead off a short lob from the Californian. Smith – the toughest man mentally in tennis – moved past Nastase 4-6, 6-3, 6-3, 4-6, 7-5 to claim the highest honor of his career.

Smith demonstrated that day – and on numerous other important occasions – that he was unshakable in the arena. He rarely lost his cool, kept playing aggressively, and seldom choked. His unruffled demeanor carried him across the finish line in more than his share of hard-fought matches against worthy adversaries.

Smith cherishes the trophy he won at Wimbledon in 1972.

As Smith told me, "I had played John Newcombe in the final the year before so I knew more what to expect than Nastase did. I felt poised and believed I was better on grass than him, but he was so talented and could hit great shots when he needed them. He missed that high backhand overhead smash to lose the match. That was lucky. Anyone could have won that match."

When Smith and the U.S. Davis Cup contingent went to Bucharest to face the Romanians in the Davis Cup final on clay courts three months later, winning seemed almost out of the question.

Facing Jan Kodes in the semifinals at Wimbledon in 1972, Smith prevailed and soon achieved his lifelong goal by taking that title dramatically over Ilie Nastase in the final.

Nastase excelled on clay while Smith was hard pressed to impose his game on the slow courts. But on opening day in the first match, a composed Smith shocked Nastase 11-9, 6-2, 6-3. After teammate Tom Gorman was beaten by Ion Tiriac in a five-set match, Smith joined forces with Erik Van Dillen to crush Nastase and Tiriac in straight sets to put the Americans ahead 2-1 in the best-of-five match series.

On the last day, Smith led off against Tiriac, knowing that winning was an imperative since the last match would have pitted a heavily favored Nastase against Gorman. The flagrantly mistaken line calls from the Romanian officials had been outrageous in every match,

infuriating the American players and captain Dennis Ralston. And yet, Smith remained a pillar of strength. Tiriac – just as he had done against Gorman – was shamelessly stalling between points and manipulating the crowd.

This fascinating battle concluded with a fifth set won convincingly by Smith at the cost of only seven points. After vanquishing Tiriac 4-6, 6-2, 6-4, 4-6, 6-0, Smith walked up to the net to shake hands and said, "I respect you as a player but I'll never respect you as a man again."

Later that day, a press conference was held at the player hotel that I attended as a 20-year-old reporter in training. As he walked to the elevator afterwards, Smith told me, "I never thought we could do it when we came over here. To beat these guys in their country on clay with so many questionable calls being made was more than I ever thought was possible."

Smith had almost single-handedly made it possible. It was his finest hour as a tennis player.

"It was the most demanding experience of my life trying to handle all the issues over there," he told me in 2009. "From the security help we needed [The Secret Service surrounded the players and captain Ralston throughout their stay after threats from the terrorist organization "Black September"), to the Romanians watering the courts every day to slow them down even more, to the linesmen maybe being related to the players, we had all sorts of things to deal with. It was the most satisfying thing by far of anything I did in tennis."

He had his share of rewarding moments in 1973 as well, especially the win over Ashe at the WCT Finals in Dallas. But he did not defend his title at Wimbledon, as the vast majority of players who were members of the ATP elected to boycott the tournament in staunch support of their fellow ATP member Niki Pilic, who had been unjustifiably barred by the International Tennis Federation for refusing to play Davis Cup for his country. At the U.S. Open, Smith reached match point in the fifth set of his semifinal against Kodes but, with darkness enveloping the stadium at Forest Hills, lost the match. A short while later, forlorn in the aftermath of a penetrating defeat, Smith sat on the steps of the clubhouse as many of his friends came by to offer condolences.

Smith's last serious chance to add another Grand Slam singles championship to his collection was at Wimbledon in 1974. Facing the evergreen Rosewall in the semifinals, Smith took the first two sets and had two match points in the third. Rosewall, 39, rallied valiantly and toppled the 27-year-old Smith in five sets. Had Smith survived, he would have met Jimmy Connors in the final. Only a few weeks earlier, he had beaten Connors on grass.

Thereafter, Smith, hampered by injuries, became less potent. He did secure a No. 2 U.S. ranking in 1974, but fell to No. 8 in 1976 and No. 7 in 1977. But he was permanently diminished by ailments. As he told me in 2024, "The injuries were tough. My arm was really hurting for about three years and I had elbow problems. I kept thinking it would get better and I would get back into it."

He did, however, remain productive in doubles, sealing his last major with Lutz at the 1980 U.S. Open when he was 33. Moreover, he kept competing favorably in Davis Cup. In total, he won 35 of 42 matches in singles and doubles combined when representing his country between 1968 and 1981.

Starting in 1986, Smith became Director of Coaching for the USTA Player Development program, remaining in that position until 1994. Year in and year out, he has taken tour groups of fans to major sporting events including the Olympics, the four majors in tennis and the British Open in golf, as part of his events company. He also opened a tennis academy in 2002 with Billy Stearns in his hometown of Hilton Head Island, South Carolina, designed to cater to about 60 young players. From 2011 to 2021 he was President of the International Tennis Hall of Fame.

Despite all his successes on the court, Stan Smith is best known for his eponymous line of tennis shoes. His friend and agent Donald Dell made a deal with Adidas in the early 1970s to put his name on one of their main tennis shoes. It eventually became a lifetime contract.

For a long time the Stan Smith tennis shoe was built strictly for tennis players, but that changed. They revised their philosophy of what the shoe could be and even added other shoes like the Stan Smith green golf shoe that was unveiled at The Masters golf tournament.

Smith is immensely proud of the role he has played in his long association with Adidas. He even wrote a book in 2018 entitled *Stan Smith: Some People Think I'm a Shoe.*

He told me in a 2021 interview for tennis.com, "The Adidas relationship has been an unbelievable chain of events. I happened to be in the right place at the right time with the right product. The shoe has embraced every segment of the population around the world – the hip-hop, the preppies, the old, the new, the kids, the older folks, men, and women. For thirty years mine has been a fashion shoe. I don't even recommend it for people who play serious tennis."

That was not always the case. At the outset, tennis players embraced the shoe and knew full well Stan Smith was a statesman in his sport. Many club players bought it because they were ardent admirers of Smith. Decades later, young people had no clue who he was. He was simply an identifying label on what they were wearing.

Smith told me in a 2024 interview for this book, "I don't have a big problem

Stan Smith leaps over the net in celebration after winning Wimbledon in 1972.

with people saying to me these days that they didn't know I played. You wouldn't necessarily expect people to be up to speed on that. I have never been that concerned with legacy. I have just enjoyed what I have done. As a player I competed hard and had the ability at the peak of my game to represent the United States in Davis Cup and win it seven times."

Learned tennis followers have known that Stan Smith has long been a man of prominence. Dell originally signed him as a client in 1970 along with Arthur Ashe, positioning them as the Arnold Palmer and Jack Nicklaus of tennis. He is one of the few great athletes who has lived his life free of controversy, reaping the rewards of a hard-earned sterling reputation.

Smith, who also secured five majors in doubles, was always humble about how he found success. As he told me in 2024, "My life has been charmed. When I was 16 I had four big goals – to be a member of the U.S. Davis Cup team; to be the No. 1 American; to win Wimbledon; and to be No. 1 in the world. Everything I did was to realize all of those goals. I am very proud of that. I think about the old saying someone made in another sport that goes 'baseball has been very good to me'. In so many ways, tennis has been very good to me."

Chris Evert came of age at the 1971 U.S. Open when she was 16 with a stirring run to the semifinals in her debut at a major tournament before losing this match to iconic countrywoman Billie Jean King.

CHRIS EVERT

Full name	Christine Marie Evert
Birthdate	21 December 1954
Place of birth	Fort Lauderdale, Florida
Major singles titles	7 French Open (1974–75, 1979–80, 1983, 1985–86); 6 U.S. Open (1975–78, 1980, 1982); 3 Wimbledon (1974, 1976, 1981); 2 Australian Open (1982, 1984)

As the 1971 U.S. Open approached, American tennis was sorely in need of a new superstar, and Floridian Chris Evert fit that bill impeccably.

Although still only 16 years old, she had the unmistakable maturity and striking composure of a champion in the making, ready to start a journey across the next 20 years which would change the face of tennis forever. A figure of considerable class and elegance, she would eventually surpass every other modern male or female player for sustained excellence over a two-decade period.

Evert came from one of America's greatest tennis families. She was one of five children raised by her devoted mother, Colette, and father, Jimmy. Jimmy Evert had been the No. 11 ranked American player in 1943 and had won the Canadian Championships four years later. He later became the highly regarded head teaching pro at the Holiday Park public tennis facility in Fort Lauderdale, Florida, which was a forerunner for emerging academies in the decades to come. All of the Evert kids reached at least the final of a national junior championship. Chris Evert was the most disciplined and dedicated player in her family, although her sister Jeanne rose to No. 9 among American women in 1974 – and joined forces with Chris to be ranked among the U.S. top five doubles teams in 1973 and 1974.

Chris Evert established herself as the youngest women's U.S.

Making her debut at Wimbledon in 1972, Evert lost a hard-fought semifinal to defending champion Evonne Goolagong.

semifinalist ever, making one patented comeback after another, turning that tournament upside down. In a fortnight tennis fans would remember for the rest of their lives, Evert, carrying herself like a wily veteran, and playing with remarkable poise, did indeed become a superstar.

At 15 in September of 1970, Evert had upended the magnificent Australian Margaret Court in a pair of tiebreakers at a small invitational tournament in Charlotte, North Carolina. That semifinal triumph happened only a few weeks after Court had become only the second woman ever to win a Grand Slam. But Evert's victory over Court was a footnote in history.

The Floridian's exploits at the U.S. Open in 1971 were another story altogether. Appearing in her first major tournament, Evert kept packing the stands for her contests, meeting the tallest of challenges, and stirring up public interest. Her first big win was against countrywoman Mary-Ann Eisel, a serve-and-volley practitioner ranked No. 4 in the United States. Eisel claimed the first set and moved in front 6-5, 40-0 in the second. From that precarious corner, an implacable Evert saved six match points and, spurred on by an enthralled Saturday afternoon crowd, rallied spectacularly to win 4-6, 7-6 (5-1 in the "Sudden Death" tiebreak), 6-1.

She followed with another tremendous comeback, knocking No. 5 seed Francoise Durr of France out of the tournament 2-6, 6-2, 6-3. Down a set again in the quarterfinals against the tenacious Australian Lesley Hunt, Evert was victorious once more 4-6, 6-2, 6-3. Her improbable journey concluded with a 6-3, 6-2 loss against the top-seeded King in the penultimate round.

As Evert told me in a 1997 interview, "The defining match for me was the one with Eisel when I saved all those match points. The ball looked like a basketball to me. But the Billie Jean match was also a defining moment. The whole thing was like a fairytale."

Planting the seeds for an outstanding future, Evert demonstrably played the game with the traits and treasures that would make her one of the greatest players ever, keeping her unerring groundstrokes extraordinarily deep, bearing down exceedingly hard on consequential points, and displaying astonishing match-playing acumen. Her anticipation from the baseline was excellent, and her timing was uncanny. She hit the ball hard, but power was not the key to her success. Evert's primary virtue was her ball control. Her feel was outstanding as she trapped adversaries in the corners and broke down their backhands with her surgically struck sidespin forehand, the most underrated stroke in her arsenal. She also could brilliantly disguise her trademark forehand drop shot, catching opponents flat-footed time and again. While the drop shot would become more prevalent in the decades to come, Evert was well ahead of her time with her adroit use of that shot. Meanwhile, her shot selection set her apart as the cagiest of tacticians, as did her excellent passing shots and lobs which were unsurpassed.

Evert's mental toughness was her strongest suit. Many experts believe she had the strongest and most disciplined mind of any woman in tennis history. Evert was impenetrable, winning a record 125 consecutive matches on clay from the summer of 1973 into the spring of 1979, demonstrating in the process that she was, almost inarguably, the greatest female clay court player in the history of the game.

Above all else, her two-handed backhand, which would become one of the best in history, was the distinctive shot in her arsenal. Evert, along with Jimmy Connors and Bjorn Borg, brought that shot into vogue.

Perhaps Evert was even more influential than Connors and Borg in popularizing the two-handed backhand, although she told me in a 2024 interview for this book, "I will never take singular credit for that. I came along in the same era as Jimmy Connors and Bjorn Borg. All three of us were teenagers then. We had equal impact on the game. After us almost everybody had a two-handed backhand. We changed the dynamic with the technique of a very important stroke and, in a sense, we changed the game."

After her surge into the public consciousness at the 1971 U.S. Open, Evert played a somewhat limited schedule in 1972 while finishing up high school, but captured four of the 11 tournaments she played including the season-ending Virginia Slims Championships at Boca Raton, Florida. She made the semifinals in her Wimbledon debut, reached the semifinals of the U.S. Open, and was ranked third in the United States. Evert turned professional at the end of 1972 when she was 18.

The following season Evert reached her first two Grand Slam finals at the French Open and Wimbledon, won 12 singles titles, established herself as the second-best player in her country behind Billie Jean King, and was No. 3 in the world. She had set the stage for a five-year run at the top of her sport from 1974–78 that carried her from the end of her teens into her mid-twenties when she took her first eight major singles championships and 62 tournaments altogether.

It was in 1974 that she took over at No. 1 in the world, won 55 matches in a row from March to September, had a breakthrough Grand Slam title run at Roland-Garros, and won her first Wimbledon while engaged to Jimmy Connors, who also lifted the trophy in London for the first time. They called off the wedding later in the year. As she told me in 2024, "The Centre Court is the most famous court in tennis. There is so much historical relevance at Wimbledon and so many important names, like Helen Wills Moody and Maureen Connolly, had their own stories and made their careers there. Winning Wimbledon made your tennis life complete. And the fact that Jimmy and I were known as the 'Lovebird Double' and were engaged at the time led to our wins being among the most publicized sports stories of that time."

Evert's first U.S. Open triumph struck an even more emotional cord for her as an American. In the 1975 final she came from behind to oust Australia's graceful and deceptively dangerous Evonne Goolagong 5-7, 6-4, 6-2 on clay at Forest Hills. She was in the midst of a record-breaking 125-match winning streak on clay.

The dominance Evert had exhibited on clay made her the clear favorite at

Following through on a forehand at the 1979 U.S. Open, Evert went all the way to the final before her 31-match winning streak at that tournament came to an end.

The sky was the limit for Evert across the summer of 1980.

the U.S. Open, adding an extra layer of pressure. And yet, from 4-4 in the second set, she won eight of the last ten games for the victory. As Evert recalls, "I remember my mother sobbing hysterically afterwards. I felt kind of embarrassed because I was more like my dad in not showing my emotions. Winning the U.S. Open for the first time had special meaning to me as an American. The crowds there were always on my side."

One other highlight from Evert's 1974–78 preeminence was another hard-fought win over Goolagong in the Wimbledon final of 1976. She prevailed over the Australian on the London lawns 6-3, 4-6, 8-6 for a second Centre Court singles title. She also expanded her streak of U.S. Open crowns in 1978 to four in a row by prevailing on the hard courts at the new Flushing Meadows site when she stopped 16-year-old sensation Pam Shriver 7-5, 6-4 in the final. But after a down-to-the-wire battle for supremacy with Martina Navratilova that season, Evert slipped to third in the world behind Martina and the 16-year-old Californian Tracy Austin in 1979.

By the time the U.S. Open came around again in 1980, Evert had lost to Austin five times in a row, starting with a setback in the final of the 1979 U.S. Open. As Evert told me in 2024, "When Tracy came on the scene she was hungrier. I had been on the tour for seven years by then and I was starting to get a little mentally tired maybe. Tracy played my game better than me at that time. She was like the next Chris Evert, and a lot of people thought she was a better version of me, maybe a little more polished than me."

In those five decisive defeats in a row against Austin, between September of 1979 and January of 1980, Evert did not take a set. In the last three matches between the two stalwart baseline players, Evert won only ten games in six sets.

Their skirmish in the semifinals of the 1980 U.S. Open – the first time they had played in more than seven months – turned into one of the most consequential matches of Evert's career.

Austin was determined to hold onto the crown she had taken from Evert the year before. She moved swiftly to 4-0 but Evert nearly turned the first set around and eventually swept 16 of the last 20 games in a 4-6, 6-1, 6-1 victory.

Evert was urged on fervently by the crowd in Louis Armstrong Stadium. "I was going for the lines," she told me in 2024, still vividly recalling the contest. "I used the drop shot a lot, came to the net, attacked her second serve, and did things I had never done in the five losses in a row I had against Tracy. I played a different brand of tennis."

That victory over Austin was a career altering development. Evert beat Czech

Hana Mandlikova in a three-set final for her fifth Open crown, finished that season back at No. 1 in the world, and, after a consistent campaign in 1981 featuring her third and last Wimbledon title run, remained the top-ranked player. But after splitting the four majors with Navratilova in 1982 and defeating the towering left-hander in the Australian Open final, she lost their next 13 head-to-head clashes.

The last of those defeats against Navratilova was at the 1984 U.S. Open when Evert took the first set and was given a thundering standing ovation from the appreciative fans before suffering one of her most bruising defeats in three sets. But she toppled Navratilova in the final at Key Biscayne, Florida at the start of 1985 and, despite setbacks in her next two meetings against the dynamic southpaw, Evert overcame Navratilova 6-3, 6-7 (4), 7-5 in an epic final at the 1985 French Open in Paris.

On a windy afternoon, Evert, who was groomed in those capricious conditions while growing up in Florida, led 4-2 in the second set and was also ahead 3-1 and 5-3 in the final set, but found herself precariously trailing 0-40 at 5-5. With characteristic poise under pressure, she held on bravely and soon closed out the match with a vintage backhand passing shot whistling sweetly down the line for a winner. At this very moment, the 5'6",

120 pound, 30-year-old Evert was surely at the peak of her physical powers.

Retrospectively, Evert placed that victory alongside or just ahead of her meeting with Austin at the 1980 U.S. Open – among her most cherished moments. As she told me in 2024, "Those two wins were one hundred percent the biggest ones for me. I was never the same player after those matches. I was a better player after overcoming my stubbornness and playing a different style against them than I had before. If I had played it safe, I never would have beaten them. It had reached the point with Martina where I had already lost the match when I walked on the court, and it was similar against Tracy."

Evert's historic rivalry with Navratilova was arguably the greatest ever in any sport. They met 80 times altogether from 1973–88, and faced each other 22 times in the majors over those 16 years, clashing 14 times in Grand Slam finals. After her long losing streak against Navratilova, Evert started reinventing herself. Her ball control and backcourt excellence remained essential attributes, but adding elements

Evert and John Lloyd playing Bjorn Borg and Mariana Simionescu in a 1980 exhibition.

to her game made Evert a better player in the 1980s. Another reason she played some of the most inspired tennis of her career in the middle of that decade was her switch from a wood racket to a larger graphite frame in 1984. In 1983, Evert became the last woman to take a major title playing with wood at Roland-Garros.

A year after the 1985 Roland-Garros triumph over Navratilova, Evert defended her title and captured a women's record seventh French Open crown 2-6, 6-2, 6-3 over Navratilova in 1986, rallying from 0-2 in the final set to sweep six of seven games with a closing flourish. That was her 18th and last Grand Slam title. She remained No. 2 in the world behind Navratilova that year, but then the fleet-footed German Steffi Graf started accelerating in 1987, moving past both Americans to No. 1 in the world. By the end of that decade, Graf turned the numbers around in her rivalry against Evert, taking their last seven contests from 1986–89 after losing the first six. Evert, realizing precisely what she was up against in facing a player almost 15 years younger, asked a friend in 1987, "What are we going to do about this girl? Steffi is just too good."

Evert playing in an exhibition when she was in her late fifties at the U.S. Open, where she had taken a record six titles during her twenties.

After not securing a major in 1987 or 1988, Evert announced that the 1989 U.S. Open would be her last tournament at the age of 34, although she did play in the Fed Cup in Tokyo,

joining Navratilova to bring victory to the United States. In the fourth round of that U.S. Open, Evert meticulously picked apart 15-year-old Monica Seles 6-0, 6-2 with a dazzling display. In the quarterfinals, however, Evert lost 7-6 (1), 6-2 to countrywoman Zina Garrison. Her decision to retire displayed wisdom.

As Evert told me, "I wanted to end my career at the U.S. Open because it was important to me to finish full circle at my country's championship. The U.S. Open at 16 was my coming-out party so to speak, and it was the first time I was exposed not only to big-time tennis but to the life I was going to lead, so it was only appropriate to have it be my last tournament."

Evert's reliability as a competitor was unparalleled. Appearing in 56 Grand Slam tournaments from 1971–89, she missed the semifinal cut only four times and garnered 18 titles including seven French Opens, six U.S. Opens, three Wimbledons and two Australian Opens. For 13 consecutive years, she took at least one of the four major titles, a record unlikely to be replicated. Across her career, she won 154 tournaments and finished with an astounding match-winning percentage of 90 percent – the highest ever recorded by a man or a woman since "Open Tennis" commenced in 1968. She spent no fewer than 19 years in a row among the American top ten from 1971–89, and nearly all of her career among the world's top four. Her consistency over the course of two consecutive decades has been unsurpassed. No wonder that Evert is considered by many to be the toughest player mentally tennis has ever known.

Evert was an outstanding role model who valued good manners and handled victory and defeat with equanimity. She told me in 2024, "Sportsmanship was just part of our family life. It was just not in my DNA to be a jerk when I lost. I wanted to be composed and not create drama, to lose the same way as I won. I realized at the end of the day it was sport."

Having said that, she added, "Something else I wanted to bring to the game was giving permission to young girls to be strong, competitive, have muscles and be tough on the court. That culture wasn't there in the early 1970s. I came along when Olga Korbut and Nadia Comaneci did. It was almost like I was saying to young girls interested in playing tennis, 'You can do this and be accepted and admired'."

Evert also prioritized how she presented herself on the court. She was proud of being a fierce competitor without sacrificing her femininity. As she told me, "I felt I could be both. I could wear ribbons in my hair,

earrings, and ruffles in my bloomers and pretty lace dresses, but still be a tough competitor on the court. It was important to me to be feminine as well as competitive, to balance it."

After Evert and Connors decided to break their engagement in 1974 since both standouts had so many worlds left to conquer on the courts, she was married twice during her career, to the British Davis Cup player John Lloyd for eight years and U.S. Olympic skier Andy Mill from 1988–2006. She started a family with Mill a few years after retiring, eventually raising three sons. Briefly, in her mid-fifties, she was married to the golfer Greg Norman. Evert established herself as one of the leading tennis commentators on television, and opened an academy near her home in Boca Raton, Florida in the mid-1990s, taking an active role alongside her brother John, who ran the operation.

Evert remained a central figure in the game long after leaving competitive tennis, conducting herself with the same class that had long been her imprimatur. Her popularity as a public figure never waned. An exemplary individual, Evert demonstrated that character is more easily kept than recovered. As renowned dress designer and tennis leader Ted Tinling once said, "Chris Evert is the most gracious champion tennis has ever had."

Connors during the US Open final in New York, 1983. Connors defeated Ivan Lendl in four sets.

JIMMY CONNORS

Full name	James Scott Connors
Birthdate	2 September 1952
Place of birth	East St. Louis, Illinois
Major singles titles	5 U.S. Open (1974, 1976, 1978, 1982–83); 2 Wimbledon (1974, 1982); Australian Open (1974)

He was a spellbinding performer, an elusive individual, and a fascinatingly complex man. He was a champion who perplexed, infuriated, and offended vast swaths of the public while simultaneously inspiring legions of loyal observers with the purity of his tennis, the depth and enormity of his fighting spirit, and his extraordinary charisma as a competitor. Few luminaries have been more evocative.

Jimmy Connors set himself apart as a player in numerous ways, winning more tournaments than any man in the modern era, capturing 109 titles between 1972 and 1989. He is the only player – male or female – to win the U.S. Open on three different surfaces. He spent no fewer than 20 years in the American top ten between 1971 and 1991. For five consecutive years – 1974–78 – he was the No. 1 ranked player in the world. Connors was revered by those who appreciated his unswerving desire to succeed at all costs. His staunch supporters regarded him as a man who redefined the place of tennis in society, as a maverick who altered the landscape of the sport irrevocably.

He could be crude and unnecessarily contentious, but no American tennis player has ever aroused so many emotions in the court of public opinion. He was responsible, more than anybody else, for expanding the

Connors plays a forehand volley at full stretch in 1977.

base of the game and captivating fans who might not have paid any attention whatsoever to tennis. Too easily forgotten, he invented the fist pump which was later copied by all of the leading players. Connors was driven by the most powerful of private engines. For better or worse, he changed tennis. Arguably, he was the single-most significant tennis player from the early 1970s into the 1990s.

Connors was molded into a phenomenal player by both his mother, Gloria, and his grandmother, Bertha, better known as "Two Mom." He told me in 1980, "I was raised in the tennis game by two women. My game is modeled after women with the compact style and the straight backswing on the forehand."

Be that as it may, Connors had unmistakable machismo on and off the court and astounding brute force in his tennis. He would eventually become just over 5'10" tall and weigh 155 pounds but, with the size of his personality and the firepower of his game, he seemed considerably bigger than that. Gloria Connors was a fine player, ranked No. 2 in the Missouri Valley women in 1942, and her mother was one of the top-ranked players in the St. Louis district. They knew the game thoroughly, guiding Connors through his childhood, giving him outstanding groundstrokes and a killer instinct.

When Connors was only eight and had been playing tennis for a few years, he was at Jones Park in East St. Louis, Illinois with his brother Johnny, his mother, his grandmother, and his grandfather. Some thugs came along playing loud music on their radio. The Connors family asked the two young men – who looked like they were in their early twenties – to turn the sound down. One of the thugs grabbed and tackled his grandfather, banging his head on the concrete court. When Gloria Connors came over to help her father, the thugs punched her and caused her to lose some of her teeth.

The cowards walked away, leaving the young Jimmy Connors permanently altered. He wrote in his 2013 autobiography, *The Outsider*, "There is blood on the court. I can't help them. I'm powerless. This day will transform me more than any other day in my life. After watching my Mom get battered, the need for revenge ran strong in me. I took my anger and used it in my tennis."

Indeed he did. Connors had the essential tools of his trade to back up his ambitions. As a junior he won seven national titles in singles and doubles combined, most importantly the National 16s singles in 1968 and the National 18s Hard Courts two years later. When he was

15, Connors moved to California to train with the renowned Pancho Segura. Gloria Connors had been the architect of his game and his most fervent booster, but she realized that Segura had the tennis brain to take her son to another level.

Segura lived up to her expectations, and Pancho Gonzalez provided his own expertise and inspiration as well. Segura kept coaching Connors through most of the period from 1972 – when Connors turned pro – to 1975. Connors had played one year of college tennis for UCLA, winning the NCAA Championships in 1971. That same year he rose to No. 5 in the United States.

It took Connors little time to make his presence known on the pro tour. He won six titles and 75 matches in his rookie 1972 season and climbed to No. 3 in American tennis. His 1973 season was outstanding. Connors took 11 singles titles including the U.S. Pro Championships where he beat both Stan Smith and Arthur Ashe. Later that year he captured the South African Open over Ashe. He was co-ranked No. 1 in the U.S. with Smith.

Connors was ready in 1974 to celebrate the greatest year of his career. He moved through that season with growing self-conviction, taking the Australian Open early in the year, winning his first Wimbledon title in July, and wrapping up the summer with a triumph at the U.S. Open. Altogether,

Connors would win 15 tournaments and 94 of 98 matches. By winning all three major championships that he played and backing it up with 12 more titles – even if some of those tournaments had relatively weak fields – Connors had, by all accounts, a seminal season.

In the finals of Wimbledon and the U.S. Open, Connors ruthlessly rejected the graceful 39-year-old Australian Ken Rosewall, winning their Wimbledon title-round appointment 6-1, 6-1, 6-4 and succeeding even more decisively 6-1, 6-0, 6-1 at the U.S. Open in the most one-sided men's final in the history of the tournament. Connors had just turned 22 when he won that match and his speed, power, depth, and clean ball-striking were breathtaking. His flat two-handed backhand became one of the most formidable strokes of all time, his return of serve was outstanding, and the completeness of his game was commendable.

Connors wrote in his book regarding his two gems against Rosewall, "I was up against the people's favorite, Ken Rosewall, and once again, I reached perfection, only quicker. To reach such a peak once in your life is lucky, but to experience the sensation twice within two months is truly amazing, and it never happened for the rest of my career."

The left-hander had a respectable first serve which he moved around the box skillfully, and a decent kick second-delivery that kept him out of trouble. But his strongest suits were his blockbuster returns and his searing shots off the ground which always seemed to land inches from his opponent's baseline. His flat two-handed backhand was the best in the game. Making his tennis all the more remarkable was the fact that for most of his career he used the Wilson T2000 steel racket, known for its trampoline effect. Most players gained power but lost control with that frame, but Connors found the range with his flat groundstrokes without missing much at all.

During the middle of that 1974 U.S. Open, I sat down with Connors in the locker room upstairs at the West Side Tennis Club in Forest Hills, and interviewed him for *World Tennis* magazine. He had a discernible edge to his comments. Perhaps part of it was that he had been barred from the French Open that year because over the spring and summer he participated in World TeamTennis for the Baltimore Banners.

A triumphant Connors after stopping John McEnroe in a five-set Wimbledon final in 1982.

Connors leaping for an overhead at the French Open in the early eighties.

WTT participants were not allowed to play the French Open. Had he played in Paris and prevailed, Connors would have become the first man since Rod Laver in 1969 to win the Grand Slam.

He had some fascinating things to say in our interview. Asked how he felt about Arthur Ashe's comment that as an American he valued the U.S. Open in some ways even more than Wimbledon, Connors fired back, "Why would he say that? Because I won Wimbledon? Everybody says how great it is to win Wimbledon. Then I win it, and everybody tears it down. Everybody said in the past that Wimbledon was the biggest title in the world. I win it and I still say it is the biggest title in the world. If Arthur had won Wimbledon, ask him what title he thinks is biggest."

Connors was simply not one of the boys. He refused to join the Association of Tennis Professionals (ATP), telling me "They want to rule the game. They want to tell players what to do and where to play and when to hit good overheads and when to miss them. I don't want anybody to come in and take over the game to dictate and to rule. The idea is if I want to take two weeks off, I take two weeks off."

That was not a popular stance with most of his fellow players who believed in the ATP, nor did it help that his manager Bill Riordan was deliberately instigating baseless lawsuits in those days against Ashe, the ATP and other tennis organizations. But Connors – spurred on by the feisty Riordan who operated like a boxing promoter – made some of the animosity from colleagues work in his favor in that golden 1974 season. The following year, slightly out of shape and perhaps overconfident, he still made it to the finals of the Australian Open, Wimbledon and the U.S. Open, and won nine titles, but his aura of invincibility was gone, and Ashe stole his thunder at Wimbledon. The Connors luster was largely lost.

In 1976, however, he played with renewed vigor. Connors was prolific, purposeful, and highly professional. He was victorious at 12 tournaments and won 100 of 109 matches, rising once more to the top of his nation's ranking list. Unlike 1975 when he officially finished second behind Ashe in his country, Connors returned to No. 1 in the U.S. The highlight of his season was winning a second U.S. Open. He had come through on the grass at Forest Hills in 1974 but now, two years later, he took the title on clay with one of his signature career triumphs. Connors defeated Sweden's Bjorn Borg 6-4, 3-6, 7-6 (9), 6-4 in a stirring final, saving four set points in the critical third set tiebreak with some of the boldest and biggest clutch-hitting of his career.

That victory reverberated throughout the inner chambers of his sport because Borg had won his first of five straight Wimbledon's earlier that summer, and the Swede was unassailable on clay. When I asked Connors in a 1980 interview to assess the weight of that third-set performance that led him to victory over Borg at the 1976 U.S. Open, he responded, "That tiebreaker was probably the best tennis I will ever play under such pressure conditions."

Connors was riding high after that scintillating 1976 season, but was brought down to earth over the next few years, largely by the swiftly improving Borg, along with Argentina's southpaw wizard Guillermo Vilas. In 1977, a determined Connors rallied from 0-4 in the fifth set of the Wimbledon final against Borg to reach 4-4, 15-0, but never won another point as the Swede fended him off 3-6, 6-2, 6-1, 5-7, 6-4 in a bruising setback. Two months later, he lost to Vilas 2-6, 6-3, 7-6 (4), 6-0 in the U.S. Open final despite having two set points in the tenth game of the third set. Connors took the season-ending Masters title at New York's Madison Square Garden with a riveting final-round win over Borg, and remained so dependable, week in and week out – with a 69-11 match record and eight titles – that he remained at No. 1 in the ATP computer rankings on the year-end list. But all of the game's authorities placed either Vilas or Borg at the top.

Borg routed Connors in the 1978 Wimbledon final 6-2, 6-2, 6-3, but Connors retaliated by casting aside Borg 6-4, 6-2, 6-2 in the U.S. Open final, recording his last win ever over the Swede on the hard courts at Flushing Meadows. Connors would lose to Borg in their last ten meetings from 1979–81 to finish with an 8-15 record against his great adversary. By winning 68 of 74 matches and ten tournament titles in 1978, however, Connors celebrated a fourth year in a row as No. 1 ranked player in the world. But the times were changing with the emergence of New Yorker John McEnroe, a combative individual to his core. Connors remained a hard-nosed fighter but by offering some conviviality to the fans during big matches he created a different image for himself.

Now Connors was not only hounded by Borg, but McEnroe at the age of 20 surpassed him in 1979 as well. He toppled Connors with alarming ease 6-3, 6-3, 7-5 in the semifinals of the U.S. Open. Connors dropped to No. 2 in the U.S. despite taking eight titles, and lagged behind his fellow left-hander again in 1980 and 1981 when he won ten tournaments in the two years combined.

But 1982 was a time of extraordinary revival for Connors as he turned 30. For the first time since 1974, he won Wimbledon and the U.S. Open in the same year after not taking any Grand Slam titles from 1979–81. He was three points from losing the Wimbledon final to McEnroe when trailing 3-4 in the fourth set tiebreak, but rallied ferociously to win a blockbuster 3-6, 6-3, 6-7 (2), 7-6 (5), 6-4. Connors was pointing to the crowd charismatically in a manner reminiscent of the boxer Muhammad Ali when he was one game away from victory to signal that he was going to beat his countryman, and thereafter the fans urged him on effusively. He wrote of that monumental

In 1978 Connors celebrated a fifth consecutive year at No. 1 in the world.

Turning 39 in the middle of the 1991 U.S. Open, Connors, amazingly, reached the semifinals.

match in *The Outsider*, "I had to come up with a way to pin McEnroe to the baseline: to change my serve by putting more juice on it, flattening it out, hitting it deeper. If he managed to get his racket on it, my forward momentum would allow me to get to the net quicker. He wouldn't be expecting that. [I knew] if I could rattle Mac and keep the match close, I could beat him."

Connors also realized that the atmospherics at Wimbledon, with more emphasis on decorum, did not fit his personality the way raucous crowds at the U.S. Open did. As he told me in 1994, "Everything Wimbledon was, I wasn't. How I ever played well there and won the tournament twice is beyond me."

In any case, at the 1982 U.S. Open, Connors upended the powerhouse Ivan Lendl in a four-set final. Winning seven tournaments that season and 78 of 88 matches, he was crowned "World Champion" for the year by the International Tennis Federation.

He wrestled the No. 1 American ranking away from McEnroe as well.

A year later, Connors claimed his eighth and last Grand Slam title by defending his U.S. Open title with another four-set, final-round victory over Lendl at 31. Connors advanced to the semifinals at the French Open, the final of Wimbledon and the penultimate round at the U.S. Open in 1984, but lost on all three occasions to McEnroe. Although he was still formidable, his decline after wrapping up 1985 at No. 4 in the world was apparent. He did garner the No. 1 U.S. ranking in 1986 and 1987 with McEnroe struggling, and then was the second best in the U.S. in 1988 behind Andre Agassi. He slipped to No. 8 among Americans in 1989 and then needed wrist surgery in 1990. His career was seemingly just about over, but characteristically he refused to give up.

Remarkably, Connors found some of his old magic in 1991. Competing in his 21st U.S. Open, Connors, buoyed by euphoric audiences cheering his every move, enjoyed what he regarded as the finest fortnight of his long career as he turned 39. Down two sets to love and 0-3, 0-40 in the third set of the opening round match against Patrick McEnroe, he somehow prevailed at 2 a.m. after 4 hours and 18 minutes.

The old lion was roaring again. Connors, determined to make this a rousing last hurrah, won his next two matches comfortably and then on Labor Day, across a long afternoon, he made another magnificent comeback against fellow American Aaron Krickstein, winning that round-of-16 clash 3-6 7-6 (8), 1-6, 6-3, 7-6 (4) after trailing 2-5 in the final set. He then cut down the Dutchman Paul Haarhuis in four sets for a place in the semifinals at 39 before losing to No. 4 seed Jim Courier. But the psychic rewards he reaped after such a dazzling and unexpected run were more than enough for Connors. Over ten years later, he told me when we crossed paths at Wimbledon, "Those were the best eleven days of my career at the 1991 U.S. Open."

Connors played on the ATP Tour sporadically until April of 1996. By then, he was helping to manage and play on the senior tour. He was not the greatest American tennis player of all time, although he belongs high on the list. But he was surely the best competitor in the history of his country, a man with an enduring mission, and a champion of rare force and magnetism. Connors was an American hero to some, an antihero to others. Regardless of where you stood, the immortal Jimmy Connors is irreplaceable in the realm of American sports.

Navratilova rallied from 2-4 down in the final set to defeat Evert in a memorable 1978 Wimbledon final.

Martina Navratilova

Full name	Martina Navratilova
Birthdate	18 October 1956
Place of birth	Prague, Czechoslovakia
Major singles titles	9 Wimbledon (1978–79, 1982–87, 1990), 4 U.S. Open (1983–84, 1986–87); 3 Australian Open; (1981, 1983, 1985); 2 French Open (1982, 1984)

Billie Jean King is renowned for raising the profile of women's tennis in the embryonic stages of the Open Era. Chris Evert inspired legions of fans with her wide range of commendable qualities including style and unparalleled consistency. Those two icons changed the game irrevocably. So, too, did Martina Navratilova, who thoroughly reshaped the sport with her own outstanding characteristics.

Raised in the former Czechoslovakia before defecting in 1975 and proudly becoming a United States citizen six years later, Navratilova evolved into an astonishing physical force. In the 1980s, she lifted off-court training to a new level altogether.

Guided by the basketball player Nancy Lieberman, the left-handed Navratilova did extensive training in the gym and exacting drills on the court. Through her efforts to turn her physicality into a weapon, Navratilova was ahead of her time.

She secured a women's Open Era record 167 singles titles across her career along with 177 doubles championships to earn widespread recognition as perhaps the greatest all-round player in the history of women's tennis. She claimed a record nine singles titles at Wimbledon and 18 singles majors. Altogether, this prodigious left-handed serve-and-volley stylist amassed 59 majors in singles, women's doubles, and mixed doubles

Navratilova at the U.S. Open in September 1982.

combined, second among all players behind Margaret Court of Australia. This versatile performer even won a doubles Grand Slam alongside Pam Shriver in 1984.

Navratilova was a champion through and through, and arguably the best volleyer ever in women's tennis, right alongside King. Her quicksilver lateral movement at the net was mind-boggling.

Born in Prague, her parents divorced when Martina was three years old but her mother, Jana, remarried prior to Navratilova's fifth birthday. Mirek Navratil did not feel like a stepfather to Martina; she thought of him as her second father. In the Czech language and culture, girls take on the feminine letters "ova" at the end of their name. Until the age of 10, she was Martina Subertova, but that year she changed her name to Navratilova.

Navratilova's grandmother once defeated the mother of 1962 Wimbledon finalist Vera Sukova at the Czech Nationals. When very young Navratilova learned to ski. She took gymnastics as a kid and played ice hockey and soccer. But by the time she was ten, after getting increasingly serious about it in preceding years, she was playing tennis every day.

In that period she started taking lessons from the highly regarded former Czech player George Parma at his facility. His guidance during her formative years was crucial. Around that time she went to the Sparta Sports Center

in Prague and watched the dazzling Australian left-handed maestro Rod Laver play. As Navratilova wrote in her 1985 autobiography, *Being Myself,* "If ever there was a player I wanted to copy, it was Laver. He was my greatest sports idol."

Navratilova captured the Czech Nationals in 1972 at 15. The following year she made her first journey to the United States to play tournaments, and got to the quarterfinals of her maiden major at the French Open. But 1975 was the defining season for Navratilova. She played over 100 matches, took three titles and concluded that year at No. 3 in the world.

Within a few days of her semifinal loss to Evert at the 1975 U.S. Open, Navratilova – who had philosophical differences with the Czech Tennis Federation regarding when and where she could play and how much of her prize money she could keep – defected to the United States at 18. She wrote in *Being Myself,* "I got to Forest Hills [in 1976] and all the memories of 1975 came flooding over me … the fears of being kidnapped by Communist officials, the worries about where I would live. I put a lid on the emotions surrounding my defection for a whole year."

When I spoke to her for this book in October of 2024 about the 1975 defection, Navratilova elaborated, "You don't realize what a big deal it is when you are in it. I didn't think of myself as a star because I was from a communist country, and the press didn't pay that much attention to me until after I defected. When you are 18 you figure things will work out. You don't think of the monumental consequences. You are self-absorbed. I regret that I had to do it, but don't regret doing it. There is a difference. It was necessary for me to do it if I wanted to be in charge of my life and pursue my dreams."

It took some time for Navratilova to adjust to living in a new country, but she did that in short order. In the early 1980s she was outed by an American reporter about her gay lifestyle, which surely had financial consequences and resulted in fewer endorsements. Navratilova had several high-profile relationships and eventually married her longtime partner Julia Lemigova in 2014.

In any event, her 1976 campaign on the court was less stellar than the previous one. She got to the semifinals at Wimbledon but lost in the first round of the U.S. Open when she was about 20 pounds overweight. By 1977 she was much trimmer and got back to No. 3. In the years ahead, her dietary discipline was unmistakable.

Navratilova hit the first peak of her career in 1978, winning seven consecutive tournaments and 37 indoor matches in a row on the Virginia Slims circuit.

She then made a spirited comeback from 2-4 down in the third set against Evert for her first Wimbledon and major singles title, winning five of the last six games in a 2-6, 6-4, 7-5 triumph. At the end of that season she was ranked No. 1 on the official WTA computer. The following season, she stopped Evert once more in the Wimbledon final, and remained at No. 1. She was still not a U.S. citizen in 1979, but Navratilova garnered the No. 1 American ranking for the first time.

She dropped to world No. 3 in 1980 and then in the spring of 1981 was trounced 6-0, 6-0 in the final of the tournament at Amelia Island, Florida on clay by Evert. It was at that time when Lieberman began working with Navratilova on her fitness for a consequential three-year stretch.

In July of 1981, nearly six full years after her defection, Navratilova was sworn in as a U.S. citizen in Los Angeles, California. Less than two months later, she lost the final of the U.S. Open 1-6, 7-6 (4), 7-6 (1) against Tracy Austin, but the prolonged ovation she received as the tears streamed down her face at the presentation ceremony was something to savor. Seldom had she been showered with so much affection from the American fans.

At the end of that season, Navratilova's growing resilience was evident in the final of the Australian Open against

Evert. On a windswept afternoon in Melbourne, she was ahead 5-1 in the third set on the grass courts at Kooyong, but Evert boldly made it back to 5-5. Navratilova refused to surrender, took two games in a row and closed out a stunning 6-7 (4), 6-4, 7-5 victory over her greatest rival. It was a testament to her growing tenacity and temerity.

That victory in Australia set the stage for the five most prolific years of her career from 1982–86. In fact, they were almost surely the five best years consecutively of any woman in the history of tennis in terms of volume and sustained brilliance. In that magnificent span, Navratilova appeared in 84 tournaments and won 70 of them. She was victorious in 427 of 441 matches, losing a grand total of 14, collecting 12 of her 18 major singles crowns in that period.

Navratilova not only benefitted from the alliance she had with Lieberman, but from two outstanding coaches in that period. Renee Richards – a transgender athlete with a brilliant tactical mind along with technical savvy who was also a left-hander – coached Navratilova from 1981 into 1983. She made Navratilova better from the backcourt, more compact on the forehand volley, and smarter strategically. Mike Estep – a Texan who reached the top 100 in the world – took over as Navratilova's

coach from 1983–86 and urged her to attack incessantly. Also contributing significantly during those golden years was Robert Haas, who transformed her diet by mandating no fats, oils, butter, red meats, and sugar, while recommending loads of vegetables, pasta, grains, bread, and skim milk. It was a recipe for success. Eating with such discipline – and working diligently on exercise machines, weightlifting, and running – enabled Navratilova to be sprightlier on the court.

Navratilova told me in 2024, "Nancy Lieberman made me realize how much better I could be. Getting my U.S. citizenship was important. I was able to come out on the court and not worry about anything and do everything I could to win. Getting the coaching first from Renee Richards and then Mike Estep was unbelievably helpful to me. I hit the sweet spot there. I got my act together and then felt almost unbeatable."

Her year-by-year output was astonishing. In 1982, Navratilova captured her first French Open, and won her third Wimbledon by defeating Evert in the final. For the season, she posted a 90-3 match record, securing 15 titles. In 1983, she had the finest year statistically of her career, winning 86 of 87 matches, taking 16 tournaments including her breakthrough U.S. Open title over Evert.

Navratilova returned to Prague to lead the US Federation Cup team to victory over the Czechoslovakian team in 1986.

Eating with such discipline – and working diligently on exercise machines, weightlifting and running – enabled Navratilova to be sprightlier on the court.

Speaking of that sparkling season, Navratilova said, "I treated every match as if it was the Wimbledon final. I didn't differentiate. Nobody can plan on losing one match all year. It just happened but it wasn't ever a goal."

In 1984, the 5'8" Navratilova was victorious in 78 of 80 matches, taking 13 titles altogether including the first three majors of the season. She played perhaps the standout match of her career to beat Evert 6-3, 6-1 in the final of the French Open, toppling her premier rival for her lone win in their four title-round contests at Roland Garros.

At the end of that season, her bid to sweep all four majors for an official calendar year Grand Slam fell narrowly short when she lost to Czech Helena Sukova 1-6, 6-3, 7-5 in the semifinals of the Australian Open. Her modern record of 74 consecutive match triumphs ended that day.

As she told me, "I was going for [a record] seven Grand Slam titles in a row in Australia. In my mind I had already won a Slam since I had done four in a row at the French Open of 1984. Trying to get seven straight was creating the pressure for me, not going for the calendar year Grand Slam. But it was a great year. I lost in my first tournament of the year and did not lose again until the last one. That might never happen again. It's pretty cool."

Navratilova in 1985 remained almost freakish in her excellence, winning 84 of 89 matches, collecting two more majors and taking 12 titles in total. Her 1986 season was even better as Navratilova claimed victory in 89 of 92 matches and 14 of 17 tournaments. She secured a fifth Wimbledon title in a row and a third U.S. Open, but those exploits were overshadowed by Navratilova's return to her former nation for the first time since she defected 11 years later.

In the summer of 1986, Navratilova joined Evert and longtime doubles partner Pam Shriver in Prague, representing the United States in the Fed Cup international team competition. Navratilova had first become eligible to play for her new country in 1982 when she and Evert led the U.S. past West Germany in the Fed Cup final at Santa Clara, California.

Back in 1975 before she defected, Navratilova had spearheaded the Czechs to a 3-0 final-round Fed Cup triumph. Now she replicated that feat playing for the Americans against the Czechs in the land where she was raised. In the final round, after Evert won the opening match, Navratilova upended Hana Mandlikova 7-5, 6-1 and then joined forces with Shriver to win the doubles for the U.S. The Americans prevailed 3-0.

To longtime observers of the sport, there was no more poignant Navratilova moment.

"It was a big deal," she muses now, "You can't get too emotional about seeing your friends and family and people I had not seen for eleven years. I had a job to do – to play and to win. I wanted to show how well I could play and represent my new country well. At the same time I was playing against Czechoslovakia in the finals. It was hard for Hana Mandlikova playing against me. I felt bad for her. The people were cheering for me. But this was not a tennis thing. It was both emotional and political support I was getting from the people. That whole trip was a total emotional roller coaster, all ecstasy or agony with nothing in between."

The landscape changed in 1987. Germany's Steffi Graf improved exponentially, winning the French Open over Navratilova before losing their final-round skirmishes at Wimbledon and the U.S. Open. Graf was ranked No. 1 in the world but Navratilova was the top-ranked American for the sixth consecutive year.

Across the next few seasons, Graf was spectacular, becoming the third woman ever to win the Grand Slam in 1988, collecting three of the four biggest titles the following year. Navratilova managed to win nine tournaments in 1988 and eight more in 1989 as the preeminent American player, but was a distant No. 2 in the world behind Graf.

Nevertheless, she won her first singles major in three years at Wimbledon in 1990, securing a record ninth title and last Grand Slam event in singles on those hallowed grounds. Four years later, Navratilova fell one set short of a tenth Wimbledon singles triumph, losing to Spain's inspired Conchita Martinez.

For all practical purposes, her career was coming to a close as she turned 38 in 1994. Navratilova played an intended farewell tournament at Madison Square Garden in New York at the season-ending Virginia Slims Championships, losing in the first round to Gabriela Sabatini. She had spent 19 years in a row (1975–93) among the top five in the world and 20 consecutive seasons in the top ten. She garnered the No. 1 U.S. ranking 13 times and stood among the top three for 16 straight years (1979–94).

Through most of her career, Navratilova's storied 1973–88 rivalry with Evert carried women's tennis to the hilt. The peaks and valleys of that series were unparalleled. Evert had the upper hand decidedly from 1973–78, winning 20 of their first

Navratilova during the finals of the women's singles at Wimbledon in 1990.

Navratilova had plenty to smile about in this 1990 Wimbledon final as she defeated Zina Garrison for a record ninth singles title at the shrine.

24 contests before Navratilova defeated her in their 1978 Wimbledon final. Up until the latter stages of 1982, Evert was still ahead 30-18 before Navratilova took their next 13 duels. Navratilova ultimately won 43 of their 80 skirmishes, with 60 of those meetings in finals. They met 22 times at the majors with Navratilova winning 14 – including 10 of their 14 finals.

Making it all the more remarkable were their contrasting styles and temperaments. As Navratilova told me in 2024, "We had the quality and the quantity. That will never happen again. Nobody will ever play eighty matches in a rivalry like ours. I am proud of that. I knew I had to get in better shape if I wanted to compete with Chris and be more steady from the baseline to set up my attack at the net. Then, when I started beating her more regularly, she changed rackets and got in better shape. We made each other better tennis players. I knew it was special while we were going through it, but not fully until it was over."

Navratilova played singles at Roland-Garros and Wimbledon when she was almost 48 in 2004, but lost in the first round at Roland-Garros and the second round in London. The fact remained that she was still an outstanding doubles player, as confirmed by her triumph alongside Bob Bryan at the 2006 U.S. Open in mixed doubles

– five weeks before turning 50, and 31 years after taking her first major in women's doubles. That was her final Grand Slam title, with an astonishing career tally of 18 singles, 10 mixed doubles and 31 women's doubles.

Navratilova believes she might have lasted longer had she done a few things differently.

As she told me in 2024, "Looking back, I had a single-mindedness of purpose to not just win but get better. But for eight years, until 1984 or 1985, I never had a vacation. I would have lasted longer and wouldn't have gotten burned out as I did by the end of 1986 [if I had taken vacations sooner]. It was not until '89 that I realized I was burned out. My knees were hurting. I could have had surgery and been playing pain free. I didn't know I should just stop, take a month off, and then come back. I didn't give myself permission to do that. It didn't even occur to me. That is where the single-mindedness maybe got in the way."

Martina Navratilova was a champion of the highest order, and a player who knew how to bring the best out of herself on the biggest occasions. She is one of the most formidable female athletes of all time. The touchstones of her tennis will forever be etched in the hearts and minds of all who watched her perform at her peak.

An exhilarated Austin immediately after ousting four-time defending champion Evert in the 1979 U.S. Open final.

TRACY AUSTIN

Full name	Tracy Ann Austin Holt
Birthdate	12 December 1962
Place of birth	Palos Verdes Peninsula, California
Major singles titles	2 U.S. Open (1979, 1981)

While Evert and Navratilova were the monarchs of women's tennis for a strikingly long stretch, it's easy to forget that for a while the biggest threat to their supremacy was a diminutive Californian with a steely mind, unwavering spirit, and a large heart named Tracy Austin.

The unflappable Californian was a mirror image of Evert with her finely honed ground game and calm disposition. She was a match player of the highest order. At 16, she became the youngest to win the U.S. Open by toppling both Navratilova and Evert. At 18, she upended Navratilova for a second major title on the same court.

Had she not been dealt the unkindest of hands, Austin would have shared the spotlight with her two towering rivals for years to come, and inevitably a "Big Three" of Navratilova, Evert, and Austin would have transpired, not unlike another sparkling trio decades later featuring Roger Federer, Rafael Nadal, and Novak Djokovic. Diminished by injuries, Austin was denied an opportunity to make that happen.

Austin acquired the habit of winning early, collecting 27 national junior championships from the 12-and-under division through the 18s. Her mother worked at the Jack Kramer Club near her California home. She was coached initially by the renowned Vic Braden after picking up a racket at the age of two, and later by Robert Lansdorp, who later worked with other standouts including Maria Sharapova and Pete Sampras. She was on the cover of the sport's

With astonishing poise and maturity, Austin became the youngest female player to win the U.S. Open at 16 in 1979.

premier publication – *World Tennis* magazine – when she was four in 1967.

At 14, Austin, still under five feet tall and weighing about 90 pounds, started competing in pro tournaments as an amateur in 1977 and finished that year at No. 4 in the United States. After she turned pro in the fall of 1978 at 15, she finished that season as No. 3 in the nation, surging to No. 6 in the world.

But the three best years which formed the heart of her career were from 1979–81. In 1979, Austin opened her season stylishly by defeating Navratilova indoors in the final of Washington and reaching the final of the Avon Championships at Madison Square Garden a few months

later, defeating Evert in that tournament. Then she won two prestigious clay court titles, taking the Family Circle Cup in Hilton Head Island, South Carolina before capturing the Italian Open in Rome, stopping the left-handed German Sylvia Hanika in the final after stunning the tennis world by ousting Evert 6-4, 2-6, 7-6 (4) in the penultimate round. Evert had won 125 consecutive matches on clay, but Austin rallied with temerity from 2-4 down in the final set to gain that victory.

Austin was now in the forefront of the game. She reached the semifinals of Wimbledon and then fared well over the summer on hard courts, winning the title in San Diego over Navratilova, and reaching the final in Mah Wah, New Jersey.

And so the stage was set for the 16-year-old phenomenon to take New York by storm and upend the established order at the U.S. Open. Seeded third, she was stretched to her limits by No. 11 seed Kathy Jordan in the round of 16. Austin was precariously close to losing that tense contest, but battled ferociously from behind against a formidable attacking player, and found her way to a 4-6, 6-1, 7-6 (4) victory after trailing 5-6, 15-30 in the final set. She handled Hanika easily in the quarterfinals, and then took on Wimbledon champion Navratilova.

Austin met a critical moment unhesitatingly in that contest. Serving at 5-5 in the opening set she was down 0-40 but secured the next five points in a row. That was the pivotal moment and Austin went on to prevail 7-5, 7-5. Her next assignment was even more daunting. Evert was going for a record fifth women's U.S. Open title in a row.

Many believed that the experience of nine-time major champion Evert would give her the edge over the incredibly mature teenager, but that was not the case. Twice in the opening set, Evert gained the upper hand to go up a break at 3-2 and again at 4-3, but the resolute Austin was oblivious to the immensity of the occasion, moving inexorably to victory 6-4, 6-3. No matter how many

And so the stage was set for the 16-year-old phenomenon to take New York by storm and upend the established order at the U.S. Open.

balls Evert sent back with depth and interest in the long rallies, Austin had all the right responses. Not once did she blink with nearly 20,000 seated in Louis Armstrong Stadium and millions more watching on television. At 16, she broke the record of 1951 champion Maureen Connolly and established herself as the youngest U.S. Open champion ever.

Reflecting on winning that title so convincingly, Austin told me in 2024, "Life was moving so quickly. I had been a ball girl for Chris at the Virginia Slims of L.A. when I think I was eleven years old, played her at Wimbledon when I was 14 for the first time, and beat her for the first time at Madison Square Garden that spring of 1979. It is a process and also a physical thing where you have to get stronger, and a tennis thing – you have to get good enough. I wasn't intimidated, like 'Gosh I could win the U.S. Open' or 'Wow, this could change my life,' which is hard to explain."

Austin conveyed her recollections to me with deep humility, adding, "If I was in that same position now in the final of the U.S. Open my legs wouldn't move because I would be thinking about the wrong things, like 'You are trying to beat Chris Evert who has won this tournament four times and you can win your country's major and become a Grand Slam champion.' I wasn't thinking about any of those things at the 1979 U.S. Open. I was just trying to be very clear about how I needed to play. The calm was always there, and looking back at it now in 2024 it seemed like I was able to compartmentalize each point. It surprises me now that I had that clarity in my mind. I was almost in a trance."

Austin's mind was absolutely and almost uniquely orderly. Her coach Robert Lansdorp had been working with her for nearly ten years by then, and his view was that Austin had uncanny competitive instincts that guided her through the minefields of her matches. As he told Susan Adams of *World Tennis* magazine days before Austin won that breakthrough U.S. Open, "Tracy seems to pick the right shots instinctively. That you cannot teach. You just show her the possibilities; give her a couple of ideas and she will determine when to hit what shot. I know that because she outguesses me."

Clearly, 1979 was a year of affirmation for Austin as she remained No. 3 in the U.S. behind Navratilova and Evert but that also meant she was No. 3 in the

world. Austin won seven titles, toppled Evert six times in eight matches – winning the last four of those clashes without dropping a set – and prevailed in five of her 11 duels with Navratilova. To face the top two players 19 times combined in one year was proof of her growing stature and reliability.

Therefore, it was no surprise when she made it to No. 1 in the world in the spring of 1980 on the official WTA computer. She told me, "Today getting to No. 1 is now on everybody's radar but in 1980 I was just thinking about doing my best and trying to win the next tournament. I remember my Mom leaning over and whispering to me after I won a match when I was playing at Hilton Head that the WTA had told her I was going to be No. 1. That was huge because the thought of one day being ranked No. 1 in the world first came into my mind when Billie Jean King came to our club when I was in the fourth grade and they told us she is No. 1 in the world. I thought to myself that being the No. 1 tennis player in the world was quantifiable. There is no No. 1 lawyer or No. 1 surgeon. So I thought it was pretty cool."

Austin had a magnificent season in 1980 with a career-best 12 tournament victories and an 89-7 match record. She won the prestigious Avon Championships in New York at Madison

Defending her title at the 1980 U.S. Open, Austin advanced to the semifinals before losing to Chris Evert.

Square Garden over Navratilova. She captured titles on clay, indoor carpet, grass, and hard courts.

Recollecting that spectacular season in 2024, Austin told me, "Winning eleven or twelve tournaments in a year is insanity. They make a big deal now if you win five. I didn't know what was normal. You are just putting one foot in front of the other and everything is happening so fast. It is just a whirlwind. I didn't win a major but I did get to No. 1. I also won the Wimbledon mixed doubles with my brother John that year which was a highlight."

But her body was starting to break down, especially her back, which forced her out of competition from the middle of January into the middle of May in 1981. In that stretch she went to at least five doctors to determine what was going on, but none of them could solve the problem. "Nobody could figure

Child prodigy Austin, competing in Los Angeles at the age of nine, was an outstanding junior player.

out what it was or how to heal it," Austin told me in 2024.

Nevertheless, she played her way back into form. By the time she returned to the 1981 U.S. Open, Austin was soaring. Only about three months shy of turning 19, she had essentially reached full height at 5'5"and weighed about 110 pounds, which contributed to more searing shots off both sides and an ability to set the tempo more from the back of the court. After losing in the quarterfinals of Wimbledon to Pam Shriver, Austin pieced together

a 28-match winning streak that carried her from summer into autumn.

She would win four tournaments in a row during that stretch, most significantly her second U.S. Open. On her way to the final as the No. 3 seed, Austin swept her six matches at the cost of only 24 games. She confronted the No. 4 seed Navratilova in the title-round contest on a day of high stakes, ineffable drama, and capricious winds.

The fast-charging Navratilova was unshakable in taking the opening set 6-1 before Austin retaliated to claim the second set with her patented passing shots and impeccably struck low returns, yet her left-handed adversary was unrelenting on the attack. Austin served for the match at 6-5 in the third set but, despite a 40-15 lead and three match points in that 12th game, she could not get across the finish line. For the first time ever, a major final was decided in a final set tiebreak.

In an immaculate tiebreak performance, Austin, who had been peppering away at Navratilova's weaker backhand the entire match, won three points with precise down-the-line forehands. Two of those shots landed for winners and the other forced Navratilova into an error. Without making a single mistake in that match-concluding sequence, Austin won the tiebreak seven points to one and completed a hard earned 1-6, 7-6 (3), 7-6 (1) victory.

Austin told me in 2024, "That match was kind of emblematic of the year. Martina could absolutely smother you with her game, especially at the net with her swashbuckling style and deep volleys mixed with drop volleys. What an incredible athlete she was. I probably had to dig deeper than I ever had to in any match to win. It would have been easy the way Martina was playing to mentally disappear because everything was going against me."

Reminded that Navratilova was struggling that day with her forehand volley – particularly the high one – Austin says, "People say she missed some forehand volleys but there are things in a tennis match that are overt and things that I guess are covert where you don't see them. Maybe what some people couldn't see was all the cumulative pressure I was putting on her by keeping my shots deep, keeping the scoreline close, and with my consistency and passing shots. I was doing my best against a great player."

At the end of that memorable season, Austin was victorious at the season-ending Toyota Series Championships in East Rutherford, New Jersey. She defeated Evert in the semifinals, and came from behind to beat Navratilova in the final. It was her seventh and last title of an abbreviated season. It was also the last time she played tennis on such a lofty level. She finished that year narrowly behind Evert at No. 2 in the world on the WTA computer. Bud Collins wrote in the *USTA Yearbook* about Evert, Austin, and Navratilova, "Has the game ever seen a more formidable trio on the scene at the same time? Doubtful."

Thereafter injuries were her constant enemy, making it impossible for Austin to play often or well enough. In 1982 she dropped to No. 4 in the world, winning only one of 13 tournaments, playing only 46 matches. The following year she played 32 matches, did not win a tournament, and dropped to No. 9.

Austin told me, "The same mentality that got me to No. 1 made me come back too quickly from injuries. I would get shoulder tendinitis and I got plantar fasciitis which is a major problem. I felt I was losing time so I would work too hard and another injury would crop up. It was a vicious cycle."

From 1984–92, Austin was not even ranked as her injuries kept her out of circulation. She kept going into 1994 when she played her last two majors at 31, but her body was uncooperative.

As she told me, "It is so hard when your whole life you have a purpose and you are thinking about working on this today, or traveling tomorrow, and then you have the back, or you have got plantar fasciitis, and you are doing physical therapy for the rest of the day. You feel kind of lost. I didn't have things to sink my teeth into as I had my whole life. I wasn't able to do what I wanted to do, which was to get back on the court and play tournaments."

But as disconcerting as it was for Austin to be sidetracked by injuries, that could not compare with a car accident she experienced on 3 August 1989, which could have been fatal. She was playing World TeamTennis in New Jersey. Driving away from her hotel at 10 a.m., she went into the left-turn lane and the last thing Austin remembered was a white van hurtling toward the intersection around 65 mph. She blacked out. When she woke up, Austin recalls screaming, "I am paralyzed. I am paralyzed!" Soon an ambulance picked her up and drove her to the hospital. Testing showed that Austin had a bruised heart and spleen from the seat belt. It was also discovered that her tibia plateau was crushed.

She soon had surgery to take bones from her hip and graft them into her knee. For a year, she had to endure physical therapy five days a week, but her knee was too damaged. After about two hours of practice the pain was severe. She made a final bid in 1994 to restore her career, but that was futile.

The 1989 accident was traumatic. As she explained to me in 2024, "Overall there was a one percent chance of me living through that accident. Just the sheer impact of that makes it a miracle that I survived. If you looked at my car you would ask how did anybody live through that?

That changed my life forever. I think
I am a pretty happy person because
I feel like all of this is just a bonus."

Despite her monumental misfortunes,
Austin found joy in raising three sons
with her husband Scott Holt. She was
proud to have accomplished so much
in her career including rising to No.
1, winning two U.S. Opens and taking
30 career titles before she turned 20.
Maureen Connolly's horseriding accident
ended her career just shy of 20, but
she had won the Grand Slam by then.
Monica Seles was stabbed in the back by
a deranged spectator in 1993 when she
was 19 and then her psyche changed.

Austin's mentality resembled both
champions. Had she been healthy
across the 1980s, she would have likely
picked up many more prestigious
titles. Moreover, she would have been
competing for a long time against Evert
and Navratilova in a three-way battle for
supremacy before battling in the latter
stages of the decade against Graf.

Despite her short time at the top,
Tracy Austin's impact and influence on
the game was immense. The potency
of her quietly imposing personality
on court, her match-playing acumen,
the tenacity she brought to the
arena – all of these things make her
an American tennis immortal.

As she muses, "In the late 1970s
with the tennis boom, you had Borg,

*A beaming Austin takes back the U.S.
Open trophy in 1981.*

Connors, McEnroe, Chrissie, and
Martina. I guess you can throw in
that other character who was a young
American with pigtails who made it more
interesting. I felt good that somebody
else had joined the party. I am super
proud that in a short period of time a lot
happened with me that was impactful.
I was so glad to be a part of that."

Exultant after his win over Bjorn Borg in the 1981 U.S. Open final.

John McEnroe

Full name	John Patrick McEnroe Jr.
Birthdate	16 February 1959
Place of birth	Wiesbaden, Germany
Major singles titles	4 U.S. Open (1979–81, 1984); 3 Wimbledon (1981, 1983–84)

While Jimmy Connors altered the culture of American tennis with his anti-establishment outlook, the same can be said for fellow left-hander John McEnroe. McEnroe was the quintessential New Yorker, six-and-a-half years younger than Connors but an individual with a much larger sense of irony.

They detested each other but, deep in their souls, realized how much they had in common as fellow left-handers refusing to be held captive by officials in the tennis universe. These two charismatic champions rebelled against authority and appealed to a new constituency of fans.

But McEnroe differed fundamentally from Connors in one crucial respect. He genuinely loved playing for his country in Davis Cup competition. He poured his heart and soul into that forum, and his achievements possibly surpass anyone who has ever represented the United States. In 12 years of playing for his country between 1978 and 1992, McEnroe won 41 of his 49 singles contests and 18 of 20 doubles duels.

He played on five victorious American squads and his unbridled spirit was never manufactured. Davis Cup was made for McEnroe, and vice versa. He accomplished mightily on his own, capturing seven Grand Slam singles titles between 1979 and 1984, and nine majors in doubles from 1979 to 1992. He amassed 77 singles and 77 doubles crowns on the ATP Tour, more combined than

McEnroe in 1979 demonstrates his remarkable athleticism on the forehand side.

any other man in the Open Era. But Davis Cup meant more to him than anything else. Quite a bit more.

McEnroe was raised by a father and mother always striving for high standards. He was born in Germany, where his father, John McEnroe Snr, was stationed with the U.S. Air Force, but the family returned to New York when John was nine months old. His father was a lawyer who managed him throughout his playing career and boosted him immeasurably as a parent and cheerleader. His mother, Kay, raised John and his younger brothers Patrick and Mark strictly and fairly. John went to Stanford University for one year and won the NCAA Championships in 1978. Patrick went to Stanford in the eighties and was a three-time All American. He won the French Open doubles title in 1989, reached the semifinals of the 1991 Australian Open in singles and played for the U.S. Davis Cup team. Later, Patrick succeeded John as the American Davis Cup captain, serving in that role for ten years, guiding his team to victory in 2007.

John started playing tennis at his local club when he was eight. His junior years were productive, including eight national title triumphs in singles and doubles. He was guided for a while by renowned Australian Davis Cup captain Harry Hopman, who was teaching the game by then in the U.S.

The turning point for McEnroe was in 1977 when he astonishingly reached the semifinals of Wimbledon as a qualifier at 18 before losing to Connors in four sets, one month after winning the French Open mixed doubles title alongside Mary Carillo. That was when his game was evolving.

As McEnroe explained in his 2002 autobiography, *You Cannot Be Serious*, "It wasn't until Wimbledon in 1977 that I felt strong enough to serve-and-volley … That was when it all came together for me."

At the end of that season, McEnroe was ranked No. 10 in the United States. He was ready to play professional tennis but wisely went that fall of 1977 to Stanford University for one year. McEnroe then turned pro not long before Wimbledon in 1978 where he lost early.

But at the 1978 U.S. Open, the No. 15 seed McEnroe wisely addressed some ongoing back pain. As he wrote in *You Cannot Be Serious,* "My lower back was still tight and for some reason … I decided to turn completely sideways when I served. I noticed the difference immediately: it relieved the pain … Not only was my back getting better but people were having a tougher time reading my serve."

McEnroe made it to the semifinals of that U.S. Open before losing to Connors. He closed the year spectacularly, taking five singles titles after the Open, culminating with a triumph at the season ending Masters in New York's fabled Madison Square Garden where he rallied from double match point down to overcome 35-year-old Arthur Ashe in a stirring generational battle. McEnroe was still 19.

Almost inevitably, McEnroe stamped his authority at a major tournament for the first time in 1979, ousting the defending champion Connors comprehensively in the semifinals 6-3, 6-3, 7-5 before accounting for his fellow New Yorker and friend Vitas Gerulaitis 7-5, 6-3, 6-3 in the final of the U.S. Open at Flushing Meadows in the borough of Queens, becoming the youngest man in the Open Era to take that title at 20.

"I felt like I was ready to do it," McEnroe told me on a 2018 podcast, "It was the ultimate to play Connors in the semis because he was the guy I measured myself against in terms of effort and will. In a way I was bummed that I was playing Vitas in the final. He was someone that I looked up to quite a bit. I remember thinking at the time that we were two guys from Queens growing up, say, 15 minutes from Flushing Meadows. We were not getting a whole lot of love from the crowd, but I was ecstatic to win my first major."

After ending that 1979 campaign at No. 1 in the U.S. and No. 3 in the world, McEnroe in 1980 was even more polished and professional, winning nine tournaments and a second U.S. Open in a row. But it was in a noble defeat that McEnroe enhanced his reputation.

Facing the imperturbable Borg in his first Wimbledon singles final, McEnroe competed honorably. The Swede – going for his fifth title in a row on the Centre Court – was leading two sets to one and ahead 5-4, 40-15 in the fourth set. It was double match point for the top seed. But McEnroe saved the match points with a scintillating backhand passing shot and a forehand swing-volley winner.

He broke back and soon contested the most famous tiebreak of his career.

In that stupendous sequence, McEnroe saved five more match points and took the tiebreak 18-16 as the fans saluted both players with a standing ovation. Borg trailed 0-30 on his serve in the opening game of the fifth set but conceded only one more point on his delivery the rest of the way, wrestling this historic contest away from the American 1-6, 7-5, 6-3, 6-7 (16-18), 8-6. It was one of the greatest matches of all time.

McEnroe was gallant in defeat. He would frequently mention his loss to Borg as one he cherished. As he said in a 1999 press conference, "It showed me that in losing actually that you could elevate your status. Even if you are not the winner every time, if you are a part of history it makes it okay. Being part of that match was perhaps the most exciting thing in my career. The vibrations and goodwill I get from people from that match are incredible."

Later that summer, McEnroe confronted Borg again in the final of the U.S. Open. McEnroe had beaten a swiftly emerging Ivan Lendl in the quarterfinals before somehow halting Connors in an epic semifinal. Despite losing 11 games in a row at one stage, McEnroe rallied to win the arresting encounter 6-4, 5-7, 0-6, 6-3, 7-6 (3).

A perturbed John McEnroe was trailing by two sets to one against Swedish rival Bjorn Borg in the epic Wimbledon final of 1980, but he rallied to win an unforgettable tie-breaker before losing gallantly in five sets.

Appearing at the French Open in the early 1980s, McEnroe's stance shows why his serve was always so hard to read.

Buoyed by that triumph, McEnroe built a two-set lead over Borg in the final before the Swede struck back boldly to reach a fifth set. But at 3-3 in the final set Borg, uncharacteristically, became irked by a close line call. McEnroe prevailed 7-6 (4), 6-1, 6-7 (5), 5-7, 6-4 to defend his title in style.

As he told me in 2018, "Borg wanted it so bad and sensed he could do it. I felt like I had to prove something to myself. I had gotten tired in that Wimbledon final a few months before. I wanted to show that I could hang in there and get it done, and I sensed he was feeling pressure."

Of all the majors won by McEnroe, that 1980 U.S. Open was his most impressive. He cemented his status as the top American player and was ranked second in the world behind Borg. He then had a banner year in 1981 which featured his first Wimbledon singles title over Borg, his third U.S. Open in a row where he also toppled the Swede, and another crucial role in leading the U.S. to victory in the Davis Cup for the third time in four years. McEnroe

In terms of his tennis, McEnroe wasn't getting away with anything in 1981 but was winning on the merits.

realized a lifelong dream by closing that season at No. 1 in the world.

But it was a tumultuous year for the New Yorker. Back on the hallowed grounds at the All England Club where he had played so magnificently the year before, he earned a rematch with Borg in the final and flourished, ending the Swede's 41 match Wimbledon winning streak. McEnroe came through 4-6, 7-6 (1), 7-6 (4), 6-4. In the pivotal third set, Borg had four set points when McEnroe served at 4-5 but could not convert.

Thus the fortnight ended on a high note for McEnroe after several controversial incidents in the preceding days – and even a brouhaha over his decision not to attend the Champion's Dinner. McEnroe vociferously told the umpire during his first-round match: "You cannot be serious." He later cursed at the referee.

There were more imbroglios, especially in his semifinal against Rod Frawley when he yelled "You are the pits of the world" at the umpire. The disputes he had with Wimbledon officials overshadowed his supreme creativity on the court and the importance of his historic victory. That was regrettable for him and his fans. McEnroe rankled Wimbledon officials to the point where they wanted to throw him out of the tournament, but they did not.

It was not until the 1990 Australian Open that McEnroe, well past his prime, was disqualified from a tournament during a fourth-round clash against Sweden's Mikael Pernfors. Unbeknownst to McEnroe, the penalty system had been reduced by one infraction. But he conceded in *You Cannot Be Serious* that he had been fortunate he had never been disqualified before. He was candid about pushing the envelope perilously close to default territory on countless occasions, writing, "They wouldn't default me. Why didn't they? They had a show to put on and my presence put behinds in seats. It happened at tournament after tournament: I would freak out, the umpire would hit me with a warning, a point penalty, maybe a measly fine or two (in a year when I was earning a couple of million dollars, seven hundred was pocket change), and life (and the match) would go on. If I went home, they lost money. The tournament directors knew it and the linesmen knew it. I knew it. The system let me get away with more and more."

In terms of his tennis, McEnroe wasn't getting away with anything in 1981 but was winning on the merits. The balance of power had shifted. McEnroe had surpassed Borg and Connors. He backed up his Wimbledon triumph at the U.S. Open with a virtuoso performance against Borg in the final. For the second year in a row, McEnroe and Borg were the finalists at the two biggest tournaments in tennis, with McEnroe triumphant for the third time in those four landmark contests. He came from behind to beat Borg comprehensively in New York. With the match locked at one set all and Borg ahead 4-2 in the third, McEnroe held serve and then magically released four outright winners including two topspin lobs to break back. He soared to a 4-6, 6-2, 6-4, 6-3 victory.

Borg skipped the presentation ceremony, did not speak with the media, and essentially quit tennis at 25. He would never play a major tournament again.

The Swede seemed to be not only burnt out but gloomy about his prospects against McEnroe. Their extraordinary 1978–81 series ended deadlocked at 7-7, but the Swede leaving the game so young denied the public a chance to witness more monumental clashes between two icons.

McEnroe was remorseful. As he told me in 2018, "After I played that great game to get back on serve in the third set, it was like someone let the air out of the balloon. I don't know what happened to Bjorn but he gave in and sort of tapped out. To me an even bigger disappointment was to see my greatest rival and some incredible history that we had together be cut short like that. I thought we were going to play another twenty or thirty times. I kept waiting for him to come back."

The following year, McEnroe, wishing that Borg was still around, was not the same player despite winning 77 matches and six titles to remain at No. 1 in the world. He did not win a major, losing to Connors in a five-set Wimbledon final after being within three points of victory in the fourth set tiebreak, and was beaten by a lethal Lendl in the U.S. Open semifinals. In 1983, however, he ruled at Wimbledon for the second time, and ended the year at No. 1 again.

Even McEnroe could not know that his 1984 campaign would be the very best of his career – and one of the standout seasons of any player in the modern era. He collected 13 singles titles, won 82 of 85 matches and ruled at Wimbledon and the U.S. Open. In the former tournament he dissected Connors 6-1, 6-1, 6-2 in the Centre Court final in the defining match of his sterling career.

McEnroe could do no wrong. Everything he touched turned to gold, from his precise southpaw serving, to his deft touch on the volley, to his

In 1983, McEnroe was the top-ranked player in the world.

McEnroe playing top flight senior tennis in his fifties.

impeccably timed groundstrokes. Against the greatest returner in tennis, McEnroe poured in 74 percent of his first serves, never got broken, released ten aces and no double faults, and made only three unforced errors.

British tennis writer Lance Tingay described McEnroe's flawless performance in the *World of Tennis* yearbook: "McEnroe hauled his genius to new heights and reduced Connors, twice a champion himself, to second-ratedom. In 80 minutes he took lawn tennis destruction to new limits. It was a privilege to see such perfection."

At the U.S. Open two months later, the 5'11" McEnroe took on a revitalized Connors and won a blockbuster semifinal that ended at 11.16 p.m. in the evening after five spellbinding sets. He stepped on court 17 hours later and crushed Lendl 6-3, 6-4, 6-1 for his fourth U.S. Open singles title along with his seventh and last Grand Slam singles crown.

And yet, despite piecing together a season of near invincibility, McEnroe's five-set loss to Lendl in the 1984 French Open final lingered hauntingly in his mind. It was his best chance to win the sport's premier clay court event, but Lendl rallied valiantly to win 3-6, 2-6, 6-4, 7-5, 7-5 for his first Grand Slam title.

McEnroe wrote in *You Cannot Be Serious,* "When push came to shove, I couldn't beat Ivan Lendl in the final of the French Open in the greatest year I ever had … It's the only match in which I felt I was playing up to my capabilities and lost. But he didn't beat me. I beat myself."

A year later in the 1985 U.S. Open final, Lendl avenged his 1984 final-round loss to McEnroe. At the year-end Masters tournament, McEnroe suffered an irksome loss to countryman Brad Gilbert indoors at Madison Square Garden, and, at 25, was emotionally spent.

He took a six-month sabbatical from the game into the summer of 1986, but when he returned, he was never the same again. He slipped to No. 14 in the `world at the end of 1986 and finished at No. 10 and No. 11 the next two years. He did have a revival in 1989 when he ascended to No. 4 and celebrated his seventh and last year as the American No. 1. In 1992, McEnroe at 33 made it to the semifinals of Wimbledon in singles and took his ninth major in men's doubles alongside Germany's Michael Stich on the British lawns. He then joined Pete Sampras at the end of that year to win in doubles as the U.S. beat Switzerland in the Davis Cup final.

Married to the actress Tatum O'Neal – with whom he had three children – from 1986 to 1994, McEnroe later had two daughters with rock singer Patty Smyth. They were married in 1997. His legacy is wrapped up in his individuality. No one played the game quite like he did; he was an innovator, breaking the rules of conventional wisdom frequently, serving with that unique stance that confounded his opponents, finding ways to venture forward to the net from impossibly deep positions. He was the last great singles player to compete regularly and excel in doubles and the last man to win a singles major with a wooden racket. McEnroe was the best doubles player of his era, and maybe the finest of all time. He is undeniably an American tennis immortal.

McEnroe was among the most artistic champions ever to set foot on a court, as evocative as anyone in his era, and, despite a career-long struggle to enjoy his extraordinary gifts, a man of integrity who appealed to a wide constituency of fans ever appreciative of his originality and in awe of his genius and artistry.

*Sampras becoming the youngest ever to win the U.S. Open men's title with wins over Lendl,
McEnroe and Agassi in 1990.*

Pete Sampras

Full name	Pete Sampras
Birthdate	12 August 1971
Place of birth	Washington, D.C.
Major singles titles	7 Wimbledon (1993–95, 1997–2000); 5 U.S. Open (1990, 1993, 1995–96, 2002); 2 Australian Open (1994, 1997)

The crisscrossing eras of Jimmy Connors and John McEnroe gave fans of American tennis an awful lot to shout about. They won legions of admirers with their ceaseless fighting spirit and supreme craftsmanship, sometimes offended traditionalists with their contentiousness on the court but always these two gladiators raised the profile of the game.

Pete Sampras followed in their footsteps but was fundamentally unlike his two immediate predecessors in the way he conducted himself. Sampras was cut from the same mold as Stan Smith and Arthur Ashe. He was a champion who highly valued self-restraint, and a man determined to build a reputation based on quiet dignity, decency and, above all, class. Sampras was proud to be a craftsman rather than a showman.

He was the unassailable leader of what came to be known as "The Greatest Generation" in the history of American tennis. All of these accomplished players – including Andre Agassi, Jim Courier, and Michael Chang – emerged in the late 1980s and achieved voluminously through the nineties, collectively capturing 13 majors. Sampras captured 14 Grand Slam championships and ultimately established himself as the greatest American male tennis player of all time.

This magnificent serve-and-volley stylist resided at No. 1 in the world for a record six consecutive years (1993–98), amassed 14 major singles

In the midst of winning his second Wimbledon title in 1994, Sampras shines with his signature running forehand.

championships between 1990–2002, which was then a men's record, and was beaten only four times in major finals. Sampras played through the heart of his career with history uppermost on his mind. Everything he did revolved

around the Grand Slam tournaments; anything else was secondary.

It was therefore fitting that this immensely athletic, 6'1" American would take the tennis world by storm as the No. 12 seed at the 1990 U.S. Open when, at 19 years and 28 days old, he became the youngest man ever to win the United States Open with triumphs over No. 6 seed Thomas Muster of Austria, three-time champion Ivan Lendl, four-time victor John McEnroe, and No. 4 seed Andre Agassi. It was on the hard courts in New York when Sampras declared his greatness with that string of spectacular victories.

Down the stretch, Sampras seemed to take his game to loftier levels every time he stepped on the court improving in every match, leaving his accomplished opponents dumbfounded by his poise and perspicacity on the big stage. He came from behind to defeat the tenacious, left-handed Muster in four sets, overcame Lendl in five sets, held back McEnroe in four sets, and capped it all off with a resounding 6-4, 6-3, 6-2 victory over the heavily favored Agassi.

As Sampras told me in 1997 when reflecting on that magical fortnight in 1990 for a piece in *Tennis Week* magazine, "It was very similar to Boris Becker winning Wimbledon at 17 [in 1985]. The U.S. Open is where I made my mark as a 19-year-old kid. It was like a fairytale and I really didn't quite know the impact I was going to have on the game."

Indeed he did have issues adjusting to his newfound status. Understandably, Sampras was not able to live up to his phenomenal 1990 run in New York over the next couple of years. He struggled in 1991 to revisit the might of that moment. Countryman Jim Courier upended Sampras in the quarterfinals of the 1991 U.S. Open, and Sampras wrapped up the season at No. 6, one down from the previous year.

The following year he captured five tournaments and ascended to No. 3, but suffered a devastating defeat in the U.S. Open final against Sweden's stoical Stefan Edberg. Sampras served for a two-sets-to-one lead but squandered that opportunity with a couple of double faults. His 3-6, 6-3, 7-6 (5), 6-2 loss led to the kind of self-reflection that was ultimately beneficial.

As he told me for the biography *Pete Sampras: Greatness Revisited*: "For those couple of years from the 1990 U.S. Open that I won until I lost the Edberg final in 1992, I wasn't sure what I wanted out of the game. I am not sure if I was one hundred percent willing to sacrifice. I lost that third set in the tiebreak and something popped. My energy in the fourth set completely went away. I felt like I went through the motions. For months after that I looked myself in the mirror and asked myself what I wanted. My outlook on my tennis and my life completely shifted after kind of packing it in during that fourth set against Edberg. That 30 minutes changed the next ten years for me. The rubber hit the road. It all shifted for me."

Forcing himself to face the music enabled Sampras to develop layers of resilience that would carry him through the rest of his career. He ended 1992 as the No. 3 player in the world. Starting in 1993, Sampras was determined to amass as many majors as possible and become the sport's preeminent player. The pivotal point in his career was his triumph at Wimbledon that year, which he secured by knocking out the defending champion Agassi in a five-set quarterfinal, three-time former champion Boris Becker 7-6, 6-4, 6-4 in the penultimate round, and then Courier 7-6 (3), 7-6 (6), 3-6, 6-3 in the final for his long-awaited second major and first Wimbledon title.

Sampras was impenetrable with a playing style designed to smother the opposition. His serve was arguably the best in the history of the game, powerful and extraordinarily precise, smooth, and elegant. His second serve was so potent and biting that opponents felt as if they were facing two first serves. That splendid serve was the cornerstone of his game, but Sampras had another signature shot with his explosive running forehand, and his skills at the net improved tremendously and were always underestimated. On top of that, his conventional overhead was magnificent and his leaping smash a work of art. Sampras was the most complete player of his era, easily the finest athlete of them all, a virtuoso performer electrifying audiences everywhere he went with his speed and athleticism.

After taking that first Wimbledon title, Sampras was ready to rule the sport. He claimed a second U.S. Open title a few months later, stopping the tenacious Chang in a crucial four-set quarterfinal under the lights and eventually ousting the Frenchman Cedric Pioline in the final at Flushing Meadows. He finished the year at No. 1 in the world. His 1994 campaign was similarly impressive as Sampras prevailed at the Australian Open for the first time with a final-round victory over countryman Todd Martin, and won Wimbledon again with his cleanest run ever across the fortnight in Great Britain. He dropped only one set in seven matches and played one of his

greatest ever grass court matches in the final to stop the huge-serving Croatian Goran Ivanisevic 7-6 (2), 7-6 (5), 6-0.

Sampras celebrated another tremendous year in 1995, winning a third Wimbledon in a row – the first American man ever to realize that feat – a third U.S. Open, and spearheading the U.S. Davis Cup team triumph over Russia in Moscow with two singles wins and one in doubles, almost single-handedly carrying the Americans to victory.

That was perhaps the most emotional year of Sampras's career. At the Australian Open in Melbourne – where he lost to Agassi in the final – his coach and close friend Tim Gullikson was sent to the hospital and was later diagnosed with brain tumors. He would die about 16 months later. Gullikson returned to the U.S. prior to Sampras's quarterfinal contest with Courier. He rallied from two sets down to reach a fifth set when a fan screamed, "Do it for your coach." Sampras cried at a changeover and later had difficulty setting up to serve as the tears welled up in his eyes.

Courier – an old friend and former doubles partner – looked across the net and said, "Are you all right, Pete? We can do this tomorrow." That remark struck a chord with Sampras, who recovered his intensity, serving aces through his tears on his way to a stunning comeback triumph. Tom Gullikson, twin brother of

Sampras shakes hands with Andre Agassi after toppling his chief rival in a pivotal 1995 U.S. Open final.

Tim Gullikson, was Sampras's Davis Cup captain and briefly coached him late in his career. Tom told me in 2019 for *Pete Sampras: Greatness Revisited*, "That was just raw emotion that Pete showed when he cried. In a weird way, it was like the first time people saw that side of Pete because everybody thought he was a tennis machine who didn't have emotions."

The second moment adding clarity to the sensitivity in Sampras was right after he beat Agassi in the 1995 U.S. Open final. That was one of the most important wins of his career because Agassi had beaten him three of the four times they had clashed earlier that season, and he had won four tournaments and 26 matches in a row

The Sampras serve shown here in the mid-1990s at the U.S. Open.

leading up to this landmark duel with his fellow American. Sampras lifted his game immeasurably to meet that grandiose moment and came through 6-4, 6-3, 4-6, 7-5. Moments later, Sampras was waiting for the presentation ceremony to begin when he spoke unprompted from his heart into a CBS television microphone at courtside. Knowing an ailing Tim Gullikson had been watching the match at his home on television, Sampras said, "That was for you, Timmy. I'm coming to Chicago and I am going to beat you at some golf in a couple of days. Thanks for your help, bud."

In 1996, Sampras came back to New York for the U.S. Open having not won a major all year. He played Spain's guileful backcourt player Alex Corretja in the quarterfinals. It was as debilitating a battle as he would ever endure. Early in the fifth set tiebreak, Sampras vomited on the court but somehow saved himself from match point down to win. The American fans were chanting his name in the latter stages, cheering him on fervently, willing him to victory. He somehow survived

a harrowing ordeal 7-6 (5), 5-7, 5-7, 6-4, 7-6 (7). Sampras came back after two days off to defeat Ivanisevic in a four-set semifinal and then eclipsed Chang in straight sets for his fourth Open title.

That win was instrumental in allowing Sampras to stay at No. 1 in the world for the fourth year in a row, and a few months later he underlined his supremacy by beating Becker in an epic five-set final in Hannover, Germany at the ATP Finals.

Life was never as easy for Sampras as many observers perceived it. He battled ulcers and dealt with thalassemia, a low red blood cell count leaving him susceptible to deep fatigue on the most oppressive days. But he always soldiered on. In 1997, he collected two more majors including a second Australian Open crown and a fourth Wimbledon title in five years. That Wimbledon was the greatest serving tournament of his career: he was broken only twice in 118 service games. Across that stellar season he won eight tournaments and remained the world's top player.

Never as consumed with his ranking as much as he was with Grand Slam titles, Sampras realigned his priorities in 1998. He had finished the previous five years at No. 1 in the world to tie the record set by Connors (1974–78). Sampras realized how much breaking that record would mean historically. Preoccupied with that goal, he had an uneven season and won only four tournaments. But he was victorious at Wimbledon for the fifth time, defeating Ivanisevic in a tense five-set final-round duel.

Establishing himself as the year-end No. 1 for the sixth year in a row was singularly fulfilling for Sampras. As he told me in 2019, "I had just this one chance to do it, to break one of the all-time toughest records. Quite honestly, sitting here at age 47, looking back on that 1998 year, it feels like a great achievement. I know how hard it is to stay at No. 1 and to do it for six straight years is a beast. Who knows if that record will ever be broken?"

But arriving at that destination left him depleted. Sampras took time off at the start of 1999 but shined brightly once more at Wimbledon. In the final, he beat Agassi 6-3, 6-4, 7-5. Locked at 3-3 in the first set but behind 0-40, Sampras brilliantly served his way out of danger and never looked back. He peaked propitiously on his favorite court in the world in the masterpiece match of his career.

Sampras took that triumph in London and roared through the summer with tournament wins in Los Angeles and Cincinnati. He came into the U.S. Open as the favorite but hurt his back in practice and had to withdraw. Nevertheless, despite having to recover from a herniated disc and missing most of the autumn tournaments, he won in Hannover again at the prestigious ATP Finals, taking apart Agassi in the title-round meeting as comprehensively as he had done at Wimbledon.

Back at the shrine in 2000, Sampras injured himself during a second-round victory and played the rest of that tournament hobbled by tendinitis in his lower leg and ankle. And yet, despite needing injections before his matches and not being able to practice, he moved into the final and beat the 1997–98 U.S. Open champion Australian Patrick Rafter with his parents – Sam and Georgia – in the stands for the first time to watch him win a Grand Slam tournament.

Sampras had been raised in exemplary fashion in California, where his family had moved from Maryland when Pete was seven. His parents never overreached. Sam Sampras let Pete's tutors do the tennis work. The chief architect of Sampras's game was Dr. Pete Fischer, a pediatrician who found different coaches to council Pete on the many facets of his game.

The most renowned of those individuals was Robert Lansdorp, who later worked with Tracy Austin and Maria Sharapova among others. Fischer was a tennis genius who played poorly but had an extraordinary intellect for the sport. He was responsible for Sampras switching at the age of

Leaping for an overhead as only he could, Sampras eventually landed with a sixth Wimbledon title in 1999.

Sampras embraces his father in the stands after winning a then record 13th major title in 2000.

14 from a two-handed backhand to a one-hander in the interests of long-term success as an attacking player. Fischer had a vision for how to make Sampras a towering champion.

Meanwhile, Sam and Georgia Sampras stayed in the background, but their son wanted them there at Wimbledon in 2000 and they saw history being made as Pete Sampras won a record 13th major title on the lawns in England just before darkness. He got the job done in the nick of time 6-7 (10), 7-6 (5), 6-4, 6-2 to win Wimbledon for the seventh time.

For the next two years, his motivation was diminished because he had realized his largest dreams. Sampras went more than two years without a title and endured a 33-tournament drought, although he did reach the finals of the 2000 and 2001 U.S. Opens. At Wimbledon in 2002 he suffered a startling loss to qualifier and lucky loser George Bastl in the second round. Nearly all of the critics at that point were writing his professional obituary.

Sampras, however, was convinced he could rise again on one of the premier stages. Paul Annacone had been his coach from the time Gullikson took ill at the Australian Open in 1995 until the end of 2001. Sampras thought he needed to hear other voices in the first half of 2002, working briefly with his old Davis Cup captain Tom Gullikson and then the revered Spaniard Jose Higueras. After his shocking loss at Wimbledon, Sampras reunited with Annacone over the summer.

Seeded 17th at the U.S. Open, Sampras survived an arduous five-set match with 1997 finalist Greg Rusedski in the third round, ousted No. 3 seed Tommy Haas in four sets, and then cast aside fellow American Andy Roddick under the lights in straight sets. After defeating the Dutchman Sjeng Schalken in the semifinals, Sampras found himself in a fifth career final-round skirmish at a major against No. 6 seed Andre Agassi.

Now 31, realizing he might not get an opportunity like this again, recognizing the magnitude of the moment, Sampras raised his career record to 20-14 over his worthiest rival and collected a 14th major championship – and a record-tying fifth U.S. Open men's title – by virtue of a 6-3, 6-4, 5-7, 6-4 triumph over Agassi on Arthur Ashe Stadium in front of a capacity crowd of 23,000, unleashing 33 aces in the last official tennis match he would ever play.

There had been nothing remotely comparable to this in the history of tennis with a splendid champion leaving the game after winning a Grand Slam title and going out on top. Sampras did not rush his decision to retire. He went through many months of weighing the pros and cons. Sampras returned to Ashe Stadium in 2003 for an official retirement ceremony. He had won his first and last Grand Slam titles at the U.S. Open with final-round triumphs over Agassi. Those were the bookends of an incomparable career.

The Sampras legacy? He was an exemplary sportsman, a champion of rare stature and an unflinching competitor. In the final analysis, Pete Sampras must be regarded as not only one of the greatest players of all time but the best big-match player the game has ever seen.

This 1988–89 version of Agassi reached back-to-back U.S. Open semifinals at 18 and 19 with flair and firepower.

ANDRE AGASSI

Full name	Andre Kirk Agassi
Birthdate	29 April 1970
Place of birth	Las Vegas, Nevada
Major singles titles	4 Australian Open (1995, 2000–2001, 2003); 2 U.S. Open (1994, 1999); Wimbledon (1992); French Open (1999)

No one in the history of American tennis has been more fascinating, formidable, confounding or complex than Andre Agassi. A multi-layered man determined to explore the boundaries of his personality, he spent his entire career reinventing himself.

From the 18-year-old with the long hair and blazing strokes who surged to No. 3 in the world, to his bald-headed and complicated twenties, and on to his resurgent thirties, Agassi seemed to relish exasperating the authorities. Some saw him as one of the sport's heroes with his charm, charisma and transformational playing style, while others viewed Agassi as an anti-hero striving in his unique way to put the establishment in their place. He was a singularly arresting performer.

Agassi is one of only three men to win all four majors and a gold medal in singles at the Olympic Games – joining Rafael Nadal and Novak Djokovic in that elite club. He became the only man since "Open Tennis" was established in 1968 to win the U.S. Open as an unseeded player in 1994. Agassi – whose longevity is confirmed by the fact that he played at his beloved U.S. Open for 21 consecutive years (1986–2006) – was enduringly ubiquitous. His journey through the minefields of professional tennis was remarkable as he collected eight "Big Four" prizes and reached the pinnacle at No. 1 in the world for a total of 101 weeks.

Andre Agassi, shown here holding the trophy, stunned both himself and the tennis world when he won Wimbledon in 1992 to claim his first major title on the British lawns.

Perhaps Agassi was destined to land among the elite. His father, Mike, an Olympic boxer for Iran, settled in the United States and raised Andre and his three siblings, Phil, Tami, and Rita, in Las Vegas. Mike Agassi was obsessed with turning Andre into a tennis champion. As Andre Agassi writes in his 2009 autobiography, *Open,* "My father decided long before I was born that I would be a tennis player. When I was one year old … I proved my father right. Watching a ping-pong game, I moved only my eyes, not my head. My father called to my mother. 'Look', he said. 'See how he moves his eyes? A natural'."

Mike Agassi set up tennis ball machines at his home and got his son started when Andre was three, playing with a racket taped to his hand. It was clear, even then, that Agassi was a youngster with an extraordinary gift for the game.

The seminal moment in Agassi's ascent was when he was approaching the age of 14 and his dad sent him to the Nick Bollettieri Tennis Academy in Florida. Bollettieri had previously worked with leading American players including Brian Gottfried, Jimmy Arias, and Kathleen Horvath. Jim Courier came to the academy in the same period as did Agassi. The place was flooded with ambitious young individuals. Bollettieri – who would eventually

work with ten world No. 1 players – was a stringent task master. He ran his tennis operation like a military academy and Agassi was often rebellious. But the structure served him well, and by 16 he was ready to turn professional.

Agassi found his bearings in short order. In his rookie pro season of 1986, he closed the season at No. 91 in the world, and then he surged the following year to No. 25.

It was in a memorable 1988 campaign, however, when Agassi at 18 moved to No. 3 in the world on the strength of a surprising six titles. He got to the penultimate round at both the French and U.S. Opens – losing to Mats Wilander and Ivan Lendl respectively. In the former of those defeats, Bollettieri watched the duel with Wilander at Roland-Garros with me. As Wilander handily took the fifth set of that match 6-0, Bollettieri said pointedly, "You are watching a boy against a man. That is going to change soon."

He was absolutely correct, although Agassi first had to endure some growing pains. In 1989, he lost some of the effervescence he had put on display the previous year, slipping to No. 7 in the world. Agassi made inroads again and got to two 1990 Grand Slam tournament finals, falling short against Ecuador's Andres Gomez at the French Open and a sublime Sampras at the U.S. Open. Nonetheless, he moved up to No. 4 in the world that year.

Agassi reached another major final at the 1991 French Open but was outplayed by his compatriot Courier on the clay in Paris, bowing out in five sets. He dropped to No. 10 in the world but Agassi had started working with the acclaimed trainer Gil Reyes in that 1989 season. Reyes took over formally as his conditioning coach in 1990. When Agassi started with Reyes he weighed 152 pounds in May of 1989 but as Wimbledon approached in 1992, he was stronger and sturdier at 174.

Agassi had disdained playing on grass after a first-round shellacking at the hands of the left-handed Frenchman Henri Leconte in 1987. He skipped Wimbledon the next three years, leaving the game's guardians shaking their heads incredulously at his disrespect for tradition. He returned to London in 1991 for only his second appearance at the shrine, reaching the quarterfinals before losing a five-set skirmish against countryman David Wheaton.

That showing encouraged Agassi about his ability to play his best tennis on grass. With Bollettieri by his side, Agassi celebrated the fortnight of his life at Wimbledon in 1992 and spectacularly established himself as the first male player of modern times to win Wimbledon as a baseline practitioner. Seeded 12th, Agassi upended No. 4 seed Boris Becker in a five-set quarterfinal, easily dismissed three-time former champion John McEnroe in straight sets and then toppled the fearsome left-handed, big-serving Goran Ivanisevic 6-7 (8), 6-4, 6-4, 1-6, 6-4 in a stirring final.

Ivanisevic served 37 aces, but the 5'11", 22-year-old American demonstrated that his return of serve and the irresistible package of his forehand and backhand groundstrokes made him a champion who could flourish on any surface. An emotional Agassi told the media after his stunning Wimbledon breakthrough, "It is quite an irony. I really have had my chances to fulfill a lot of dreams, and I have not come through in the past. To do it here is more than I could ever ask for. You would think, this being my fourth Grand Slam final, I would go into it almost with the same snowball mentality – like 'I hope I don't lose the fourth one' – but I never felt tension.

After losing at Wimbledon in 1995 to Boris Becker, Agassi captured four titles in a row over the summer.

I just felt myself overflowing with this desire to go out there and hit shots."

Despite securing the biggest tournament in tennis, Agassi ended the 1992 season at No. 9 in the world, and fourth in the United States behind Courier, Sampras, and Michael Chang. In 1993, he won two tournaments but played only 44 matches and did not compete again after a first-round loss at the U.S. Open. An ailing wrist required surgery at the end of that year, keeping him out until late February of 1994.

He won his first tournament after the layoff in Scottsdale, Arizona but was not victorious again until he took the title in Toronto over the summer. Bollettieri and Agassi had parted ways the year before but Agassi had joined forces in the spring of 1994 with one of the game's masterminds in Brad Gilbert, an accomplished

Agassi competing at a tournament in Los Angeles only weeks before he retired at the U.S. Open in 2006.

player who in 1990 reached a career high at No. 4 in the world.

Agassi was ranked No. 20 in the world heading into the U.S. Open. Only 16 players were seeded in those days, and so he missed the cut for the first time since 1987. And yet, spurred on by Gilbert, highly charged and purposeful in every match, Agassi eliminated five seeds across the New York fortnight. A five-set backcourt duel with No. 6 seed Michael Chang in the round of 16 was the highlight, but Agassi was excellent in the final as well, removing No. 4 seed Michael Stich of Germany 6-1, 7-6 (5), 7-5 to win his first Open on his ninth attempt. He had now become a different version of himself, more focused on the basics of winning, less inclined to go for unnecessarily flamboyant shots.

As Gilbert told me shortly after Agassi won that U.S. Open for his second major title, "I always thought Andre was one

The defeat had lingering ramifications. Agassi played only three more matches the rest of 1995.

of the greatest hitters of the ball that I had ever seen, but maybe he didn't have the best strategy. Now I think Andre knows that if you go out and play at 100 percent of your capabilities with bad strategy, you can lose. But if you go out and play 60 percent of your capability with great strategy, you are going to win a lot of matches."

Agassi took that message to heart. He concluded 1994 at No. 2 in the world behind Sampras, and then played stupendously across the first eight months of 1995, opening the season with a triumph over Sampras in the final of the 1995 Australian Open. With the match locked at one set all, Sampras led 6-4 in the third set tiebreak with two set points at his disposal. Agassi rifled a trademark blazing forehand return down the line to save the first, and outmaneuvered Sampras on the second. In a signature performance, he won that match 4-6, 6-1, 7-6 (6), 6-4, taking the title on his first attempt after inexplicably skipping the tournament year after year until then. In his autobiography *Open*, Agassi reflected on his 1995 Australian Open triumph

by writing, "It is my second Slam in a row, my third overall. Everyone says it's my best Slam yet because it's my first victory over Pete in a Slam final. But I think twenty years from now I'll remember it as my first bald Slam."

Agassi seemed ready to extend his six year, eight-match winning streak against Becker when they met months later in the semifinals of Wimbledon that year but wasted a 6-2, 4-1 lead with two service breaks in hand and lost to the burly German in four sets. Nonetheless, he was unstoppable all summer on hard courts. By the time he took on Sampras in the U.S. Open final, Agassi had swept four tournaments in a row and 26 consecutive matches. But he suffered the most bruising loss of his career 6-4, 6-3, 4-6, 7-5 against his chief rival.

That defeat had lingering ramifications. Agassi played only three more matches the rest of 1995. Having resided at No. 1 for 30 weeks during the year, he finished second behind Sampras in the year-end rankings. Despite claiming the Olympic gold medal in Atlanta, Agassi, still devastated by his defeat against Sampras at the 1995 U.S. Open, lost his swagger in 1996 and dropped to No. 8 in the world. In 1997, he played only 24 official matches and performed abominably. Perhaps his marriage to the actress Brooke Shields that spring – whom he divorced two years later – contributed to his lack of commitment on the court. He even had a period when he was experimenting with the drug crystal meth which he wrote about in *Open*, and was fortunate to avoid a suspension from the ATP.

By the autumn, his ranking had dipped to No. 141. But Agassi played in two Challenger tournaments, reaching the final of the first in his hometown of Las Vegas, winning the second in Burbank, California. His willingness to play in the minor leagues of tennis as an avenue to reestablish himself in the upper echelons demonstrated that Agassi, at 27, was willing to fight his way back to where he belonged.

Despite not advancing beyond the round of 16 at all four majors in 1998, Agassi had an awfully good season, winning five tournaments and 68 of 86 matches, moving all the way back up to No. 6 in the world.

His comeback had been astonishing, but he was not satisfied.

In 1999, Agassi soared to the height of his physical and tennis-playing powers. It was the only year in his storied career that he won two major titles. The first was another of those moments when Agassi confounded his skeptics. By this stage of his career, Agassi's return of serve remained arguably the best in the history of American tennis and his ground game was as potent and purposeful as ever. But his biggest improvement was his much bigger and better first serve. Not long before the French Open, he had a shoulder injury and considered bypassing Roland-Garros, but Gilbert talked him out of it.

He went to Paris not expecting much. Seeded 13th, he came from behind to win his first-round match in four sets, and stopped the guileful Frenchman Arnaud Clement across five sets in round two. After an easy third-round win, he was down a set and a break against defending champion Carlos Moya, but rallied to win 6-1 in the fourth set. Eventually he met the Ukrainian Andrei Medvedev in the final.

Medvedev had knocked out some big names including Sampras and Brazil's Gustavo Kuerten, who had already won one of his three Roland-Garros titles. Medvedev was overpowering Agassi through two decisive sets. Midway through the second set, a rain delay allowed Agassi to benefit from a stern shouting lecture from Gilbert in the locker room, imploring him to play his brand of aggressive tennis. Eventually, Agassi did just that, making a rousing comeback to win 1-6, 2-6, 6-4, 6-3, 6-4. At long last, Agassi had secured the career Grand Slam sweep of the four majors.

After losing to a sublime Sampras in the Wimbledon final, Agassi took the U.S. Open for the second time with a five-set

An emotional Agassi spoke to the crowd in Arthur Ashe Stadium after losing in the third round of the 2006 U.S. Open in his farewell to the sport.

Joined by his wife, Steffi Graf, Agassi returned to Wimbledon for a mixed doubles exhibition in 2009 to celebrate the opening of a new Centre Court retractable roof.

In spite of another loss to Sampras at the year-end ATP Championships, Agassi reached a milestone by completing the year at No. 1 in the world.

victory over fellow American Todd Martin. Agassi knew he had been stretched close to his limits. He put his second five-set final-round win of the year at a major in perspective, saying, "The way Todd played, it was disappointing somebody had to lose. I felt like I was hanging by a thread for most of the match. It was exciting tennis. He was really executing in a way that was giving me a lot of problems."

Sitting up in the stands for Agassi's appointment with Martin, and trying to remain incognito, was none other than Steffi Graf. Graf had wrapped up her magnificent career weeks earlier after winning 22 major titles. She and Agassi were secretly seeing each other and would get married two years later.

In spite of another loss to Sampras at the year-end ATP Championships, Agassi reached a milestone by completing the year at No. 1 in the world. Agassi carried his momentum into 2000 by claiming his third Grand Slam title in the last four he had played with a second Australian Open crown. He prevailed in a tremendous five-set semifinal over Sampras – surviving 37 aces from his fellow American – after being two points away from a four-set defeat. In the final, he handled the Russian Yevgeny Kafelnikov in four sets for his lone title of the 2000 season.

He dropped five notches to No. 6. But Agassi climbed back to No. 3 in 2001 after taking a third Australian Open title.

Early in 2002, Agassi ended his partnership with coach Brad Gilbert and brought in the cerebral Australian Darren Cahill. He won five tournaments and reached the U.S. Open final, losing for the third time to Sampras in the title-round contest at Flushing Meadows. But, remarkably, he was the No. 2 player in the world that year behind Australia's Lleyton Hewitt. He was the oldest ever (at 32 years and eight months) to attain that honor since the ATP Rankings were introduced in 1973. In 2003, he captured his eighth and last Grand Slam title – and his fourth at the Australian Open. He finished that season at No. 4 after rising to No. 1 for 13 weeks at 33.

Agassi pushed on remarkably into his mid-thirties and remained No. 8 in 2004 and No. 7 in 2005, when he reached his last Grand Slam final at the U.S. Open, losing to Roger Federer in a spirited four-set clash. He was the oldest man to appear in a Grand Slam singles final since Ken Rosewall lost to Connors at the 1974 U.S. Open. For the 16th time in 20 years, Agassi was a resident of the world's top ten.

But he was playing on borrowed time. After losing to Nadal at Wimbledon in 2006 in the third round, Agassi announced he would end his career at the U.S. Open. Somehow, despite crippling back pain, he willed his way through to the third round before losing in four sets to the young German journeyman Benjamin Becker (no relation to Boris).

When it was over, Agassi tearfully addressed the audience in Arthur Ashe Stadium. After the fans gave him a standing ovation lasting about four minutes, Agassi said, "The scoreboard said I lost today. But what the scoreboard doesn't say is what it is that I have found. Over the last 21 years, I have found loyalty. You have pulled for me on the court and also in life … You have given me your shoulders to stand on, to reach for my dreams, dreams I could never have reached without you. Over the last 21 years, I have found you, and I will take you and the memory of you with me for the rest of my life."

Across his sterling career, Agassi was an inimitable individual. Bruce Jenkins of the *San Francisco Chronicle* summed him up best in a column appearing the day after Agassi's farewell match at the U.S. Open.

Jenkins wrote, "Agassi was a singular personality, someone who stood out like Marlon Brando on a movie set or Judy Garland at Carnegie Hall. Always, in good times and bad, he was a complete original."

The Williams sisters encouraging each other while joining forces in doubles at the U.S. Open in 2013.

Venus and Serena Williams

Full name	Venus Ebony Starr Williams Serena Jameka Williams
Birthdate	17 June 1980 (Venus) 26 September 1981 (Serena)
Place of birth	Lynwood, California (Venus) Saginaw, Michigan (Serena)
Major singles titles (Serena Williams)	7 Wimbledon (2002–2003, 2009–2010; 2012, 2015–2016); 7 Australian Open (2003, 2005, 2007, 2009–10, 2015, 2017); 6 U.S Open (1999, 2002, 2008, 2012–2014); 3 French Open (2002, 2013, 2015)
Major singles titles (Venus Williams)	5 Wimbledon (2000–2001, 2005, 2007–08); 2 U.S. Open (2000–2001)

When the incomparable Serena and Venus Williams were meeting in one final after another at the game's most prestigious events, former British Davis Cup player, captain and commentator John Lloyd told me, "Venus and Serena getting to the top is the greatest story in the history of the game."

"Here were two kids coming from an underprivileged – to say the least – area in east Los Angeles with a father who never played tennis and then learned it from a book, and they made good on his prediction that they would be the two best players in the world. This is the most incredible story in all of sports."

Lloyd's assessment was shared by many historians. The Willams sisters transformed tennis and sports with their success. After Althea Gibson's heroics in the late 1950s, no Black woman had claimed a major singles title victory until the Williams sisters emerged.

They became two of the all-time greats in their sport, winning a combined 30 majors in singles (23 for Serena, 7 for Venus), 14 more Grand Slam titles in women's doubles together and two each in mixed doubles. Moreover, they were both stalwart performers for their nation in the Billie Jean King Cup (formerly known as the Fed Cup) and the Olympic Games. The sisters led the Americans to victory in the 1999 BJK Cup and each took Olympic gold in singles, with Venus doing so in 2000 and Serena replicating that feat 12 years later. Together, the Williams sisters captured three gold medals in doubles as they were irrevocably reshaping women's tennis.

Richard Williams and his wife, Oracene Price, raised Venus and Serena in difficult surroundings in Compton, California, on the outskirts of Los Angeles. In 1978, Richard saw the Romanian Virginia Ruzici winning the 1978 French Open on television. He noticed that Ruzici made more than $20,000 for taking that title.

Then he had an idea. Williams had already fathered three daughters but he convinced Price to have more. First Venus was born in 1980, then Serena followed in 1981.

No one knows if the story is fact, fiction or a blend of both, but according

to Richard Williams, he was determined to turn them into champion tennis players. He first learned to play himself. Venus started at the age of four with Serena not far behind.

Richard Williams had the good sense to send his daughters to two first-rate coaches who gave them the essential stroke production they needed. Paul Cohen, a California teaching pro who worked on the tour with John McEnroe, was a big help initially. Later on, Richard Williams sent Venus and Serena to Rick Macci to work with him at his academy as the family left California to live in Florida.

Both Venus and Serena played junior tennis briefly and Venus won 63 consecutive matches in the 12-and-under division and Serena was almost unstoppable in the 10-and-under category. Thereafter, Richard Williams, going against the grain of conventional wisdom, decided it was best for his daughters to cease playing junior events. Venus was 14 in the fall of 1994 when she turned pro

In full stride walloping a backhand in 1998, Venus won her first major singles title two years later at Wimbledon.

Serena (facing camera) and Venus celebrate their gold medal victory at the 2008 Olympic Games.

and Serena played her first pro event in 1995 at 14, although she did not compete regularly until two years later.

Venus, who grew to be 6'1" and Serena, 5'9", knocked the cover off the ball from the baseline, and possessed two of the biggest and best serves the women's game had ever seen. Serena was naturally emotive and provocatively intense, confrontational with officials sometimes to her own detriment, and a phenomenal competitor with tremendous willpower. Venus was predominantly low key and reserved, almost always conducting herself with a calm assurance that made rivals quiver.

Their rise was swift. Venus made the first serious move at a major in 1997, reaching the final of the U.S. Open when ranked No. 66 in the world as a 17-year-old, losing to the esteemed Swiss 16-year-old Martina Hingis who was No. 1 in the world.

It seemed only a matter of time before Venus Williams would lead the way in her family at the majors, but Serena stunningly got there first. At the 1999 U.S. Open, after Hingis had eliminated Venus in a hard-fought semifinal, 17-year-old Serena put on a dazzling display in her first major final and cut down the top-seeded Swiss stylist 6-3, 7-6 (4). That performance was preceded by a string of notable victories. In the third round, Serena rallied valiantly from 3-5 down in the third set to topple the

Venus would not win another major for four years, through no fault of her own.

Belgian Kim Clijsters, who later took the title thrice. She then came from a set down to beat 1994 Wimbledon champion Spain's Conchita Martinez, bounced back to stop 1991–92 U.S. Open champion Monica Seles 4-6, 6-3, 6-2, and upended defending champion Lindsay Davenport in a three-set semifinal.

By the time she confronted Hingis, Serena was unstoppable. Six months earlier, Willams had beaten Graf in a captivating generational battle to win Indian Wells, signaling that she was on the cusp of something even more substantial.

Overjoyed by becoming the first Black woman to rule at a major tournament since Althea Gibson in 1958, Williams said, "It's really amazing for me to even have an opportunity to be compared to Althea Gibson. I went out and won a Slam. That's great."

Venus Williams subsequently pieced together two outstanding seasons in a row. While Serena remained formidable in that stretch, Venus was victorious at Wimbledon and the U.S. Open in 2000 and 2001. She was at her zenith, stopping Serena in the 2000 Wimbledon semifinals before halting Davenport in the final, overpowering Davenport again in the 2000 U.S. Open final, and dismissing the Belgian Justine Henin in the 2001 Wimbledon final. Capping it all off, Venus beat Serena 6-2, 6-4 in the 2001 U.S. Open final, which was the first "prime time" evening women's final in Arthur Ashe Stadium.

They were the first sisters to clash in a major final since British players Maud and Lilian Watson clashed at Wimbledon in 1884. Venus made 17 fewer unforced errors than her sister on an evening when the wind was burdensome for both players, who nevertheless showcased their overwhelming weight of shot and fleetness afoot.

Venus said afterwards, "This was our first Grand Slam final against each other. Really that's the way we would like it to be because both of us win in a way. But I hate to see Serena lose – even against me."

Venus would not win another major for four years, through no fault of her own. Quite simply, Serena took over as the queen of women's tennis. After that nighttime meeting in New York at the 2001 U.S. Open, neither Serena nor Venus reached the Australian Open final in 2002, but thereafter they were opponents in five out of six Grand Slam finals, including four consecutive finals from the 2002 French Open through to the 2003 Australian Open. Navratilova and Evert had met in finals against each other in five of six majors and six of eight altogether in 1984–85. In 1987, Navratilova played Steffi Graf in three consecutive Grand Slam finals. But never before had the same two players contested four straight major finals.

After the setback at the 2001 Open, however, Serena took over. At the 2002 French Open, she stopped Venus 7-5, 6-3 in the final. A month later, the scoreline was 7-6 (3), 6-3 for the younger sibling at Wimbledon. On they went to the U.S. Open and as the top two seeds in New York.

Venus played well in the final, but once more Serena, sporting her distinctive and audacious catsuit on court, was the game's definitive big-match player. She was serving with immense accuracy and power, finding the corners off the ground, and constructing points ruthlessly. Serving only one double fault while Venus double faulted 11 times, Serena maintained her mastery over her sister 6-4, 6-3.

The sisters closed that season at No. 1 and No. 2 in the world, and then opened 2003 standing across the net from each other in a fourth consecutive major final at the Australian Open in 2003. Serena had rescued herself colossally in the semifinals against Clijsters from 1-5 down in the final set, saving two match points and somehow succeeding 4-6, 6-3, 7-5.

On the heels of that harrowing encounter, Serena had her closest confrontation ever in a Grand Slam final against her sister. Venus served for the first set, lost it in a tiebreak, but bounced back to take the second set. At 4-5 in the third Venus imploded. Serena won 7-6 (4), 3-6, 6-4 for her fourth major in a row which was not an authentic Grand Slam but was dubbed a "Serena Slam".

The Serena-Venus streak at the majors ended in Paris when neither made it to the title round, but they met in the 2003 Wimbledon final with Serena the victor in three sets again. But the next few years were difficult for the iconic siblings, starting with the death of their half-sister Yetunde, an innocent victim in a gang-related shooting, on 14 September 2003.

As Serena Williams wrote in her 2009 autobiography, *On the Line,* "Tennis was about the last thing on my mind. It just didn't seem all that important. A lot of people ask me if maybe tennis would have been a good way to power through all this grieving, but that never occurred to me."

From 2004–2007, Serena and Venus struggled yet still rose to their share of big occasions. Serena seemed poised to win a third Wimbledon in a row but was trounced in the final by a new rival with whom she would do battle frequently

Venus serving to Serena in the 2009 Wimbledon final, which Serena won.

in the years ahead. Williams lost to the dynamic 17-year-old Maria Sharapova 6-1, 6-4 in the 2004 Wimbledon final. The Russian – who eventually won five majors and displayed a combativeness on the court reminiscent of Serena's – was a big hitter in her own right who outplayed Williams comprehensively in a Centre Court slugfest, but Serena eventually won 20 of their 22 meetings.

Going forward, Serena won the Australian Open in both 2005 and 2007 against the odds. In the former, she turned in another trademark triumph under duress, ousting Sharapova 2-6, 7-5, 8-6 in the semifinals after the Russian had three match points in the final set. In the final she captured nine games in a row to close out Davenport 2-6, 6-3, 6-0. In 2006, frequently injured, Serena descended to No. 95, but took her third Australian Open in 2007 as an unseeded player ranked No. 81, toppling six seeds in seven matches, crushing Sharapova 6-1, 6-2 in the final.

Venus, meanwhile, was victorious at Wimbledon in 2005. Seeded 14th, she produced the finest clutch performance of her career in a Grand Slam final, recouping from match point down with a brave backhand crosscourt winner in the final set against the

Serena Williams tied Chris Evert's women's record of winning six U.S. Open titles.

top seed Davenport, posting an epic 4-6, 7-6 (4), 9-7 triumph. Two years later, Venus was seeded No. 23 at Wimbledon but took the title over the Frenchwoman Marion Bartoli.

But not until 2008 and 2009 did the sisters collide again in major finals. In 2008, No. 7 seed Venus capped off an immaculate fortnight in London by overcoming No. 6 Serena 7-5, 6-4 for her seventh and last major. But the next year, No. 2 seed Serena exacted friendly revenge with a 7-6 (3), 6-2 triumph over her older sister – one

round after saving a match point against Russia's Elena Dementieva.

Two years later, Venus was diagnosed with an immune system disorder called Sjogren's Syndrome that many authorities erroneously believed might curtail her career.

Serena, meanwhile, had her own health concerns. In 2011, a dangerous blood clot in her lung was potentially life threatening. First, a serious cut in her foot had kept her off the courts for months after winning her fourth Wimbledon singles title in

Serena was relentlessly pursuing history. In 2015 she nearly became the fourth woman to win the most coveted honor in tennis – the Grand Slam.

2010, and then she had a pulmonary embolism the next year. Williams told the media in 2011, "I was on my death bed at one point."

Serena joined forces with Patrick Mouratoglou in 2012 and the wily French coach played a pivotal role in taking Serena's game to a career-high level, working with her for more than seven years. In her thirties under Mouratoglou's tutelage, Serena won ten majors and played sublimely, switching to a larger racket, changing her strings, adding variety to her game, and displaying growing tactical acuity.

In 2012, Serena outmaneuvered Poland's cagey Agnieszka Radwanska in a three-set Wimbledon final and then a few months later the highly charged American rallied from 3-5 down in the final set to defeat the world's top-ranked player Victoria Azarenka of Belarus 6-2, 2-6, 7-5 in the U.S. Open final. The following year she captured a second French Open singles title, eclipsing the defending champion Sharapova 6-4, 6-4 in a high-quality

final. Three months later, Williams beat Azarenka again for her fifth U.S. Open title. The following year she beat Denmark's Caroline Wozniacki in the final and equaled Chris Evert's record of six women's U.S. Open titles.

Serena was relentlessly pursuing history. In 2015 she nearly became only the fourth woman to win the most coveted honor in tennis – the Grand Slam. Serena dismissed Sharapova 6-3, 7-6 (5) in the Australian Open final, beat the Czech lefty Lucie Safarova in three sets for the French Open crown, and won Wimbledon over Spain's Garbine Muguruza 6-4, 6-4.

That string of triumphs took Serena into the U.S. Open as the prohibitive favorite. Playing world No. 43 Roberta Vinci in the semifinals, Serena took the first set before the Italian countered with finesse and stunning variety. With Williams's feet seemingly frozen, Vinci engineered a monumental upset, winning 2-6, 6-4, 6-4. "She literally played out of her mind," said Williams about Vinci.

Williams, who had finished four consecutive years at No. 1 in the world, dropped to No. 2 in 2016 but still won her last Wimbledon, avenging a title-round loss to the guileful left-hander Angelique Kerber at the Australian Open with a final-round triumph over the German in London.

She had tied Graf's Open Era record of 22 Grand Slam singles titles, and then broke it about seven months later when she won her seventh Australian Open over a revitalized Venus Williams 6-4, 6-4 for her last major title victory. Serena was pregnant when she claimed that crown. Alexi Olympia Ohanian Jr. was born on 1 September 2017.

Venus turned 2017 into her last big year, making it to the final of Wimbledon, finishing the season as the world No. 5 at 37. Serena made it to four more major finals as a mother – two at Wimbledon and two at the U.S. Open – in 2018 and 2019, losing to four different players.

It was the 2018 U.S. Open final which lingered longest in the public consciousness. Serena was beaten by Japan's Naomi Osaka 6-2, 6-4. Williams became incensed when umpire Carlos Ramos warned her for a coaching violation from Mouratoglou. She was later assessed point and game penalties for additional rules violations. Some believed Serena tarnished the occasion by going too far in her protestations.

That controversy occurred nine years after Serena lost to Clijsters on the same Arthur Ashe Stadium Court in the 2009 semifinals. Called for a foot fault on a second serve at 5-6, 15-30 in the second set which put her behind double match point, Williams screamed at the lineswoman, leading to a match-ending point penalty. Clijsters advanced to the final 6-4, 7-5. A commendably fierce competitor, Serena could drift into indefensible behavior.

When she was 38 and 39, in 2020 and 2021, Serena advanced to two more major semifinals. But the passage of time and lingering injuries were unbeatable opponents.

When she was 38 and 39, in 2020 and 2021, Serena advanced to two more major semifinals. But the passage of time and lingering injuries were unbeatable opponents. At the 2023 U.S. Open, Williams bid farewell. It was her 81st and final Grand Slam tournament and she lost a third-round duel in Arthur Ashe Stadium against the Australian Ajla Tomljanovic.

Asked afterward how she would like to be remembered, Williams responded, "I feel like I really brought something to tennis. Like the fight. I'm such a fighter. The different looks, the fist pumps and just the crazy intensity."

Serena had achieved so mightily that many authorities thought she should wear the G.O.A.T. (Greatest of All Time) label, although others made the case for Graf or Navratilova. But Evert – high on the list of all-time greats

Venus (right) congratulates Serena after their last major final at the 2017 Australian Open.

herself – believed Serena Williams at the height of her powers was the best ever. Although Serena's inconsistency through parts of her career was a minor flaw in her record, her longevity was outstanding. That fact is reflected in her career prize money figure of \$94,816,730. More importantly, the time span between her first and last major singles crowns – 17 years and four months – is the longest of any female player in history.

As for Venus Williams, she was not able to explore as many lofty heights as her sister, but she achieved the No. 1 world ranking, and won five Wimbledon titles in singles. By the end of 2024 she had played 93 majors and been on the WTA Tour (at least part time) for 28 consecutive years, from turning pro at 14 into her mid-forties, remaining formidable through it all.

Serena and Venus. Venus and Serena. Ever inseparable. These two immortals changed tennis forever. Perhaps Willis Thomas Jr. – who ran the Fila/Arthur Ashe Academy in Washington, D.C., – described the far-reaching influence of the Williams sisters best. As he told author L. Jon Wertheim in the 2001 book *Venus Envy*, "In Black neighborhoods, tennis isn't considered a sissy sport anymore. My kids see the Williams sisters and say, 'Hell, I want to be like them.'"

HONORABLE MENTIONS

I chose 19 players as immortals of American tennis, which was no easy task. Narrowing down the list to that number meant leaving out many worthy candidates. Here are 11 more towering figures who narrowly missed the cut, but they must be recognized for their wide range of accomplishments.

Ellsworth Vines (1911–1994)

A lanky Californian who was a powerhouse both on serve and off the forehand, Vines came into prominence just after Bill Tilden passed his peak and six years before Don Budge began approaching the top of his game. Vines was the top-ranked American player in both 1931 and 1932. In the former of those seasons, he was victorious at Forest Hills, realizing a lifelong dream by capturing the U.S. Championships, memorably defeating Fred Perry in

Ellsworth Vines

a five-set semifinal before coming from behind to beat countryman George Lott in a four-set title-round contest. The following year, he won Wimbledon with back-to-back triumphs over Australia's Jack Crawford and the Englishman Bunny Austin, serving 30 aces in an impeccable final-round display.

Vines moved on to a productive pro career starting in 1934, crushing Tilden 47-26 in their head-to-head series that year. In 1937 and 1938, he came out on top in the tours he played against Fred Perry before losing a hard-fought 21-18 series against Don Budge in 1939.

Tennis fans widely admired Vines for the way he took hold of his matches with an unruffled demeanor and the sheer might of his game.

Alice Marble (1913–1990)

Before Marble, the top women played primarily from the baseline, picking apart their rivals with their magnificent groundstrokes. Cut from a different competitive cloth, Marble established herself as the first woman to play a brand of tennis that resembled some of the leading men at that time in the way she moved up to the net so commandingly.

Alice Marble

Bobby Riggs

Marble played serve-and-volley tennis, attacking relentlessly and rushing her opponents into mistakes. She became the inspiration for future American stars including her one-time protégé Billie Jean King, winning five major titles in singles and 13 more in women's and mixed doubles combined. From 1936–40 at the U.S. Championships, she took four titles and lost only one match, beating her accomplished countrywoman Helen Jacobs in three finals. Her lone triumph at Wimbledon in 1939 was stunningly decisive; she did not drop a set in the tournament and lost only two games in her last four sets. About Marble, British historian John Barrett wrote in *Wimbledon: The Official History*, "Many say she would be the ultimate champion among all great players at their peak."

Bobby Riggs (1918–1995)

A good many tennis fans are only familiar with Riggs because of his renowned "Battle of the Sexes" appointment with Billie Jean King at the Astrodome in Houston, Texas on September 20, 1973. No fewer than 30,472 fans assembled in the arena that evening and millions more saw King defeat Riggs on television. About four months earlier, Riggs had defeated the Australian Margaret Smith Court in the "Mother's Day Massacre".

Fans witnessing those matches and following some of his theatrics in that period thought of Riggs as something of a clown. But they did not realize that Riggs was a serious player with tremendous all-round skills, a tennis player's tennis player in many ways. This American stalwart won the U.S. Championships in 1939 and 1941 and ruled at Wimbledon in 1939, claiming he won more than $100,000 after betting on himself to capture the singles, men's doubles, and mixed doubles crowns.

Riggs turned professional and realized some considerable feats, winning the U.S. Pro Championships in 1946, 1947, and 1949 with final-round wins over Don Budge. Riggs was a master strategist and a larger-than-life figure, but misunderstood by many.

Pauline Betz (1919–2011)

The best female player in the United States in the 1940s, Betz was victorious

Pauline Betz   in five of the ten major tournaments she played in her career. Four of those five triumphs took place at Forest Hills in the U.S. Championships where she was in the final six years in a row. Moreover, Betz won Wimbledon in 1946 convincingly with a final-round win over Louise Brough. Betz was then the fastest woman in tennis, and her backhand was the signature shot in her game.

But those feats are not the only reason why I include Betz here. Her larger place in the history of American tennis is what she did in 1947 to shape the future of women's tennis. Betz had lost two Forest Hills finals to her friend Sarah Palfrey Cooke. Cooke's husband, Elwood, believed that Sarah and Pauline should explore the possibility of a pro tour series against each other.

The governing body of the American game was the United States Lawn Tennis Association, now known as the United States Tennis Association. They suspended Cooke and Betz for simply contemplating a pro tour. Rather than back off their pursuit of the pro tour, Betz and Cooke leaned into it. Their decision to become professionals became official on May 5, 1947.

Betz won that tour comfortably over Cooke, and then was dominant in a subsequent series played in 1951 against Gussie Moran. A trailblazer and beacon for future generations of American women players, Pauline Betz stands among the most significant female players in the history of her country.

Tony Trabert (1930–2021)

In 1955, when he was playing the best tennis of his life and proving that he was the quintessential all-court player with an unshakable disposition, Trabert had a fantastic season. He won 18 of 23 tournaments and 106 of 113 matches, capturing three of the four Grand Slam tournaments. That capped a stellar amateur career featuring five major singles titles including two U.S. Championships in 1953 and 1955, back-to-back triumphs at the French Championships (1954–55) and one at Wimbledon (1955).

On top of that, Trabert was first-rate as a Davis Cup player, helping his country win the battle for team supremacy in 1954. He turned professional after his splendid 1955 campaign and played on honorably into the early 1960s.

Trabert is also remembered for his significant contributions to the game beyond his playing career. Starting in the early 1970s, he became a superb

Tony Trabert

commentator for CBS television for 30 years. He was an excellent captain of the U.S. Davis Cup team from 1976–80, and was President of the International Tennis Hall of Fame from 2001 to 2011.

Ivan Lendl (b. 1960)

One of my most difficult decisions in writing this book was what to do about the estimable Lendl, one of the game's all-time greats who grew up in the former Czechoslovakia in a prominent tennis family and led his country to a Davis Cup triumph in 1980 when he was only 20. Lendl eventually left Czechoslovakia and established a U.S. residence in 1984 before officially becoming an American citizen on July 7, 1992.

That was near the end of a spectacular career which ended in 1994 when Lendl was having serious back issues.

Lendl was one of the sport's most impactful athletes, taking training in the gym to another level like Navratilova, and developing a playing style that became a template for those who followed him. Lendl would take control of matches with his explosive inside-out forehand, but he also had a stinging one-handed backhand down the line and a big first serve. This earnest and unrelenting craftsman won eight major

Ivan Lendl

singles titles between 1984 and 1990, taking three French Open crowns and three U.S. Open titles, winning twice at the Australian Open, and reaching two Wimbledon finals. His run of making it to a record eight straight U.S. Open finals (1982–89) was astonishing. He won 94 career singles titles overall and finished four years at No. 1 in the world.

Lendl accomplished mightily, and I thought seriously about including him among the American immortals rather than relegating him to the honorable mention category.

Jim Courier

Jim Courier (b. 1970)

A central member of the "Greatest Generation" ever in American tennis, Courier grew up in Florida and was an exceedingly hard worker, a strikingly big hitter, a fierce competitor, and a professional through and through. A very imposing player known above all else for his incomparable inside-out forehand, he had a three-year stretch of immense productivity that made him definitively a Hall of Famer.

In 1991, he upended his old friend and rival Andre Agassi in a five-set final at the French Open for his first major title. He ended that season at No. 2 in the world and No. 1 in the United States. He opened 1992 with a triumph at the Australian Open, eclipsing Sweden's Stefan Edberg in the final, then defended his French Open crown by ousting Agassi in the semifinals and the Czech Petr Korda in the 1992 final. Courier was the No. 1 player in the world that season.

Still riding high, he defended his Australian Open title in 1993 with another final-round victory over Edberg, and then narrowly missed a third French Open crown in a row when Spain's industrious Sergi Bruguera beat him in a five-set final. Courier proceeded to reach a third straight major final at Wimbledon, where he lost to Pete Sampras. He finished that year as the second-best American player behind Sampras and No. 3 in the world. In total he won 23 total career singles titles, four majors, and led the United States to a Davis Cup victory in 1992.

Michael Chang (b. 1972)

Born in New Jersey but raised on the tennis courts of California, Michael Chang was a distinguished member of the "Greatest Generation" of American male tennis players who dominated the

Michael Chang

game during the 1990s. Chang was surrounded by luminaries like Pete Sampras, Andre Agassi and Jim Courier, but he led the way for his fellow Americans.

In 1989, Chang established himself as the youngest male player in the history of tennis to win a Grand Slam singles title when he was victorious at Roland Garros, becoming the first American man to succeed at the world's premier clay court tournament in Paris since Tony Trabert in 1955. At 17, Chang toppled top-seeded Ivan Lendl in the fourth round and later ousted Sweden's Stefan Edberg in the final of that riveting French Open – taking each of those battles in five tumultuous sets. His win over Lendl was a testament to his courage as he overcame severe cramps and even audaciously implemented an underhand serve in the final set.

Chang never won another major crown but made it to the final of three more Grand Slam championships thereafter, ascending to No. 2 in the world in 1996. Yet as an Asian American he was transcendent, inspiring future generations of players not only in the United States but across the world. At 5'9",

Michael Chang, enshrined at the International Tennis Hall of Fame in 2008, was the towering "Little Big Man" of pro tennis in his time.

Monica Seles (b. 1973)

Born in the former Yugoslavia, Seles went to train at the Nick Bollettieri Tennis Academy in Florida when she was 12 in 1986. The next few years training under Bollettieri at his facility changed her life irrevocably. Seles burst out of the blocks with gusto, becoming the youngest ever French Open champion at 16 in 1990, comprehensively changing the face of tennis with her style of play. The left-handed Seles's two-handed strokes off both sides were revolutionary as she pounded the ball uncompromisingly with extraordinary depth but also explored the short angles imaginatively.

By the spring of 1993, Seles had won eight majors altogether and was going strong before a deranged Steffi Graf fan stabbed her in the back at a changeover in Germany, which traumatically altered her life. Seles did not return to tennis until nearly 28 months later in the summer of 1995. Although she won her ninth and last Grand Slam title in January of 1996 at the Australian Open, Seles, understandably, was not the same player again, although she remained a formidable top ten resident.

Monica Seles

Meanwhile, Seles, who became a United States citizen on March 16, 1994, embraced her experience as an American, winning 15 of 17 Billie Jean King Cup singles matches for the United States between 1996 and 2002, spearheading American triumphs in 1996 and 2000. She also took the singles bronze medal at the Olympic Games in 2000 as an American.

Like Lendl, I wrestled with whether or not to include Seles in my main list of American immortals. I chose not to do so because the bulk of her best work came before she became a citizen.

Jennifer Capriati (b. 1976)

The remarkable Capriati was burdened by unreasonably high expectations early on in her career. Turning pro three weeks shy of her 14th birthday in 1990, Capriati, born and raised in Florida, concluded her rookie year at No. 8 in the world, establishing herself as the youngest to reach the semifinals at the French Open that year at 14 years and two months old. She reached the semifinals of the U.S. Open in 1991 and toppled Steffi Graf to earn the gold medal at the 1992 Olympic Games.

Jennifer Capriati

Lindsay Davenport

After a series of lackluster years, Capriati authentically realized her potential in her mid-twenties, climbing in 2001 to No. 1 in the world, winning three major titles in 2001 and 2002 and developing a strong following among American fans who appreciated her work ethic, the purity of her groundstrokes, and her extraordinary court coverage. Perhaps the defining moment of her career was overcoming Switzerland's tenacious Martina Hingis in the 2002 Australian Open final in the stifling heat of Melbourne, saving four match points on her way to a 4-6, 7-6 (7), 6-2 victory.

Capriati was one of the premier competitors in American tennis across a long span, gradually growing into her talent, leaving behind a shining legacy.

Lindsay Davenport (b. 1976)

A dignified Californian standing over 6'2" tall, Davenport never could match the mobility of the Williams sisters or Capriati, but she was a supreme ball striker who systematically set the agenda from the backcourt. Her two-handed backhand was one of the game's soundest shots and her flat forehand became one of the finest in the game. Davenport could count on her technique and the depth of her strokes to win when it mattered.

The way Davenport played from 1996–2005 was remarkable. She took the gold medal at the Olympic Games in 1996, won her first major at the U.S. Open in 1998 with an impeccable performance against Hingis in the final, cut down Graf to win Wimbledon in 1999, and secured the Australian Open title in 2000. She did not win any more majors but made it to two finals in 2005 at the Australian Open and Wimbledon.

Perhaps her greatest accomplishment was wrapping up four years – 1998, 2001, 2004, and 2005 – as the top-ranked player in the world. Davenport was single-minded in pursuit of her goals, a first-rate competitor with a strong disposition, and a champion who refused any invitation to boast about her achievements.

BIBLIOGRAPHY

Books

Agassi, Andre, 2009. *Open: An Autobiography*, Alfred A. Knopf, New York.

Ashe, Arthur with Frank DeFord, 1975. *Portrait in Motion*, Houghton Mifflin Company Boston.

Ashe, Arthur with Neil Amdur, 1981. *Off the Court*, New American Library Books, New York.

Austin, Tracy with Christine Brennan, 1992. *Beyond Center Court*, William Morrow and Company, Inc., New York.

Barrett, John, 2013. *Wimbledon: The Official History*, Vision Sports Publishing, United Kingdom.

Budge, Don, 1969. *A Tennis Memoir*, The Viking Press, New York, New York.

Collins, Bud, 2015. *The Bud Collins History of Tennis*, New Chapter Press, New York.

Connolly, Maureen as told to Tom Gwynne, 1957. *Forehand Drive*, Macgibbon & Kee, London.

Connors, Jimmy, 2013. *The Outsider*, Harper Collins, New York.

Danzig, Allison and Schwed, Peter (Editors), 1972. *The Fireside Book of Tennis*, Simon & Schuster, New York.

Deford, Frank, 1975. *Big Bill Tilden: The Triumphs and the Tragedy*, Simon & Schuster, New York.

Evans, Richard, 1982. *McEnroe: A Rage for Perfection*, Simon & Schuster, New York.

Evans, Richard, 2021. *The History of Tennis*, Rizzoli, New York.

Flink, Steve, 2020. *Pete Sampras: Greatness Revisited*, New Chapter Press, New York.

Flink, Steve, 2012. *The Greatest Tennis Matches of All Time*, New Chapter Press, New York.

Gibson, Althea, 1960. *I Always Wanted To Be Somebody*, Harper & Brothers, New York.

Heldman, Julie, 2018. *Driven: A Daughter's Odyssey.*

Jacobs, Sally H., 2023. *Althea: The Life of a Tennis Champion*, St. Martin's Press, New York.

King, Billie Jean with Johnette Howard and Maryanne Vollers, 2021. *All In*, Alfred A. Knopf, New York.

Kramer, Jack with Frank DeFord, 1979. *The Game*, G.P. Putnam's Sons, New York.

Laney, Al, 1968. *Covering the Court*, Simon & Schuster, New York.

Evert Lloyd, Chris with Neil Amdur, 1982. *Chrissie: My Own Story*, Simon & Schuster, New York.

McEnroe, John, 2002. *You Cannot Be Serious*, G.P. Putnam's Sons, New York.

McPhee, John, 1969. *Levels of the Game*, Farrah, Strauss & Giroux, New York.

Navratilova, Martina with George Vecsey, 1985. *Being Myself*, Collins, London.

Tilden, William T. 2nd, 1948. *My Story: A Champion's Memoirs*, Hellman, Williams & Company, New York.

Wertheim, L. Jon, 2001. *Venus Envy*, Harper Collins, New York.

Wills, Helen, 1937. *Fifteen-Thirty: The Story of a Tennis Player*, Charles Scribner's Sons, New York.

Williams, Serena with Daniel Paisner, 2009. *On the Line*, Grand Central Publishing, New York.

Wind, Herbert Warren (Editor), 1966. *The Realm of Sport*, Simon & Schuster, New York.

Yearbooks

World of Tennis, 1984
USTA Tennis Yearbook, 1981

Magazines

World Tennis
Tennis Week
Sports Illustrated
Tennis Championships

Newspapers

New York Times
New York Herald Tribune

Websites

www.tennis.com
www.tennischannel.com
www.usopen.org
www.usta.com

Podcasts

Courtside: The Official podcast of the U.S. Open
Advantage Connors
Court-Side with Beilinson Tennis

PHOTO CREDITS

Alamy

Back cover image, front cover images (except Serena Williams), pp. vi, 4, 14, 27, 36, 43, 47, 48, 51, 56, 68, 72, 97, 98, 100, 102, 105, 112, 124, 127, 128, 132, 134, 144, 148, 151, 155, 156, 161, 162

Getty Images

Endpapers, p.24: brandstaetter images/Hulton Archive, p.16: George Rinhart/Corbis, p.19: S.R. Gaiger/Stringer/Hulton Archive, p.20: S.R. Gaiger/Topical Press Agency, p.31: Bettmann Archive, p.34: Barratts/PA Images Archive, p.39: Bettmann Archive, p.40: Bettmann Archive, p.44: Getty Images, p.52: Jerry Cooke/Sports Illustrated, p.61: Bettmann Archive, p.62: Bob Peterson, p.78: Bob Haswell/Daily Express/Hulton Archive, p.83: Central Press, p.84: David Ashdown/Keystone, p.90: Terry Chambers/Fox Photos/Hulton Archive, p.106: Central Press/Keystone/Hulton Archive, p.109: S&G/PA Images, p.110: Tony Triolo/Sports Illustrated, p.115: Walter Iooss Jr./Sports Illustrated, p.116: Frank Lennon/Toronto Star, p.119: Jacob Sutton/Gamma-Rapho, p.122: UPI/Bettmann Archive, p.136: Art Seitz/Gamma-Rapho, p.140:

Chip HIRES/Gamma-Rapho, p.143: Focus on Sport, p.146: Walter Iooss Jr./Sports Illustrated, p.165: Steve Campbell/Houston Chronicle, p.168: Ross Kinnaird/Empics, p.178: Clive Brunskill, p.182: Getty Images/Staff, p.185: Mark Sandten/Bongarts, p.206: FPG, p.210: Timothy A. Clary/AFP, p.211: IOPP/Staff

Shutterstock

p.94, p.120, p.166

Wikimedia commons

Front cover, pp.ii, 200: Edwin Martinez; pp. viii, 93: Rob Bogaerts/Anefo; p.3: robbiesaurus; pp.6, 9, 10, 13, 20, 23, 28, 32, 75, 76: public domain; p.55: Harry Pot/Anefo; p. 58: Los Angeles Daily News; p.65: Henk Lindeboom/Anefo; p.71: Fred Palumbo (NYWTS); pp.80, 88, 152: Los Angeles Times; p.86: Gage Skidmore; p.94: Rob Mieremet/Anefo; p.131: Koen Suyk/Anefo; p.158: Rob Croes/Anefo; p.190: Chris Eason; p.192: Edwin Martinez

ACKNOWLEDGMENTS

I would like to offer my sincere thanks to a number of people who have made immeasurable contributions to my career in a multitude of ways over the years. The late Ron Bookman and Gladys M. Heldman taught me comprehensively about the craft of journalism during my years at *World Tennis* magazine. Bud Collins gave me the opportunity to work by his side when he was the premier American journalist and broadcaster. Herbert Warren Wind of the *New Yorker* magazine was steadfast in his support of me as a friend and reporter. I miss Collins and Wind immensely.

Joel Drucker is an old colleague and friend who has always been willing to share his considerable wit and sharp insights. No one has been a more loyal friend than Brad Falkner, who spent a decade at the Tennis Channel and extolled my virtues whenever he had the opportunity to do so.

My family – including my wife, Frances, son Jonathan and daughter Amanda – have all been pillars by my side. They understand my obsession with tennis and recognize why I have spent most of my life writing about it. I don't take that for granted. Nor will I ever forget the wisdom of my late father, Stanley Flink, and the role he played in shaping my career and spurring on my interest in tennis.

I also want to express my appreciation to all of the players who I have written about in this book. I have known most of them personally, interviewed many of them often across the years, and revered all of these American immortals who have contributed so mightily to the history of tennis and the lives of countless tennis fans all over the globe.

ABOUT THE AUTHOR

Steve Flink has been reporting on tennis since 1974, when he joined the staff of *World Tennis* magazine at the age of 22. Born in California and raised in Connecticut and New York, he became thoroughly immersed in watching tennis starting in 1965 when he went to Wimbledon for the first time at 12. Later in his teens, he began working behind the scenes with leading journalists and broadcasters in his field as a statistician.

Flink later served as a statistician for all of the major American television networks and as a commentator for the Madison Square Garden and ESPN networks in the 1980s and '90s. He also reported on the radio for CBS from the French Open and Wimbledon from 1982–2009.

But writing is his mainstay. He has authored four books previously including *The Greatest Tennis Matches of All Time*, and *Pete Sampras: Greatness Revisited*. After working at *World Tennis* magazine for 17 years as a writer and serving as Editor of that publication in 1990–91, he regularly wrote for *Tennis Week* magazine from 1992–2007 and for tennischannel. com and tennis.com from 2007–2021. He is currently a columnist for *Racquet Sports Industry* magazine as well as ubitennis.com. Flink has also contributed tennis pieces for *The Independent* in London and the *New York Times*.

Flink was inducted at the International Tennis Hall of Fame as a contributor in 2017 after being enshrined at the Eastern Tennis Hall of Fame seven years earlier. He lives in Katonah, New York. For more about the author, visit steveflink.com.

KRAMER · MAUREEN CONNOLLY · PAN
ALEZ · ALTHEA GIBSON · BILLIE JEAN
THUR ASHE · STAN SMITH · CHRIS EVE
MY CONNORS · MARTINA NAVRATILOV
AUSTIN · JOHN MCENROE · PETE SAM
RE AGASSI · VENUS AND SERENA WILLI
LDEN · HELEN WILLS MOODY · DON B
KRAMER · MAUREEN CONNOLLY · PAN
ALEZ · ALTHEA GIBSON · BILLIE JEAN
THUR ASHE · STAN SMITH · CHRIS EVE
MY CONNORS · MARTINA NAVRATILOV
AUSTIN · JOHN MCENROE · PETE SAM
RE AGASSI · VENUS AND SERENA WILLI
LDEN · HELEN WILLS MOODY · DON B
KRAMER · MAUREEN CONNOLLY · PAN
ALEZ · ALTHEA GIBSON · BILLIE JEAN
THUR ASHE · STAN SMITH · CHRIS EVE
MY CONNORS · MARTINA NAVRATILOV
AUSTIN · JOHN MCENROE · PETE SAM
RE AGASSI · VENUS AND SERENA WILLI
LDEN · HELEN WILLS MOODY · DON

CHO GONZALEZ · ALTHEA GIBSON · B
CHRIS EVERT · JIMMY CONNORS · MAR
NROE · PETE SAMPRAS · ANDRE AGASSI
ELEN WILLS MOODY · DON BUDGE · JA
NZALEZ · ALTHEA GIBSON · BILLIE JEAN
RT · JIMMY CONNORS · MARTINA NAV
E SAMPRAS · ANDRE AGASSI · VENUS A
MOODY · DON BUDGE · JACK KRAMEL
EA GIBSON · BILLIE JEAN KING · ARTH
NNORS · MARTINA NAVRATILOVA · TRA
DRE AGASSI · VENUS AND SERENA WIL
BUDGE · JACK KRAMER · MAUREEN CO
ILLIE JEAN KING · ARTHUR ASHE · STA
INA NAVRATILOVA · TRACY AUSTIN ·
US AND SERENA WILLIAMS · BILL TILD
ER · MAUREEN CONNOLLY · PANCHO G
HUR ASHE · STAN SMITH · CHRIS EVE
ACY AUSTIN · JOHN MCENROE · PETE S
IAMS · BILL TILDEN · HELEN WILLS MO
NNOLLY · PANCHO GONZALEZ · ALTHEA
SMITH · CHRIS EVERT · JIMMY CONNI